Music Express

LESSON PLANS, RECORDINGS, ACTIVITIES, PHOTOCOPIABLES AND VIDEOCLIPS

Compiled by **Maureen Hanke**

with **Ana Sanderson, Stephen Chadwick** and **Emily Haward**

Illustrated by **Alison Dexter**   Edited by **Emily Haward** and **Sheena Roberts**

ndon

Contents

First published 2003
Reprinted 2003
by A & C Black Publishers Ltd
37 Soho Square, London W1D 3QZ
© 2003 A & C Black Publishers Ltd
ISBN 0 7136 6230 1

Teaching text © Maureen Hanke, Ana Sanderson,
and A & C Black 2003
Unit headings, unit summary text, learning objectives and
outcomes © Qualifications and Curriculum Authority, 2000
CD/Videoclips compilation © A & C Black 2003
Edited and developed by Emily Haward and Sheena Roberts
Designed by Jocelyn Lucas
Cover illustration © Alex Ayliffe 2002
Inside illustrations © Alison Dexter 2003
Music setting by Jenny Fisher
Audio CD sound engineering by Stephen Chadwick
Videoclips filmed and edited by Jamie Acton-Bond
CD-ROM post production by Ian Shepherd
at Sound Recording Technology

Printed in Great Britain by Caligraving Ltd, Thetford, Norfolk

A & C Black uses paper produced with elemental chlorine-free
pulp, harvested from managed sustainable forests.

Introduction

About Music Express

Music Express provides teaching activities that are imaginative, inspiring and fun.

It has been written especially for classroom teachers. It is:

- user-friendly;
- well planned;
- fully resourced, and
- no music reading is required.

Using Music Express as a scheme of work

National Curriculum

Music Express fulfils the requirements of the Music National Curriculum of England, of Wales and of Northern Ireland and the 5-14 National Guidelines for Scotland.

Learning with *Music Express*, children will gain a broad and balanced musical education. They will:

- learn about and sing songs from around the world including the British Isles;
- learn about music from different periods and genres;
- enjoy music lessons with a balance of listening, composing, performing and appraising.

A steady progression plan has been built into *Music Express*, both within each book and from one year to the next, ensuring consistent musical development.

Opportunities are identified throughout for evaluating the children's work and monitoring their progress.

The English QCA scheme of work for music

Music Express is based on the structure of the QCA scheme of work. It uses the same unit headings, and provides activities for all the learning objectives and outcomes.

The teaching activities in *Music Express* have been drawn from and inspired by A & C Black's extensive classroom music resources.

The units

There are six units in each book. Below is a list of the units in *Music Express Year 6*, as described by the QCA:

Cyclic patterns
'This unit develops pupils' ability to perform rhythmic patterns confidently and with a strong sense of pulse.'

Roundabout
'This unit develops children's ability to sing and play music in two (or more) parts. They explore the effect of two or more pitched notes sounding together – harmony. They experiment with clusters of pitched notes and discover which combinations are 'comfortable' (concords), and which 'clash' (discords). They sing rounds and experiment with melodic ostinati to provide accompaniments. They play drones and single note accompaniments.'

Journey into space
'This unit develops children's ability to extend their sound vocabulary, including the use of ICT, and to compose a soundscape.'

Songwriter
'This unit develops children's ability to compose a song with an awareness of the relationship between lyrics and melody.'

Stars, hide your fires
'This unit develops and demonstrates children's ability to take part in a class performance with confidence, expression and control.'

Who knows?
'This unit provides an opportunity for children to develop and demonstrate the musical skills, knowledge and understanding achieved in years 5 and 6.'

There are three activities per lesson which may be taught in one longer music lesson, or over three shorter lessons to suit your timetable.

Planning

The CD-ROM

The CD-ROM provides a medium term plan and six, weekly lesson plans for each unit. These may be printed out to go in your planning folder.

Whilst it is not necessary when teaching the activities to have the lesson plan alongside, it contains useful information for preparing your lesson. This includes:

- the learning objectives and outcomes;
- a list of the resources and minimal preparation you will need to do before the lesson;
- a list of the musical vocabulary appropriate to the lesson (see glossary for definition);
- a suggestion of ways to provide differentiated support for particular activities;
- a lesson extension – a suggestion for taking the lesson further with individuals or the whole class. (The extension activities are particularly useful when teaching a mixed year-group class as they extend the older and/or more able children.)

The book

The book provides step-by-step teaching notes for each lesson. These are written to be as easy to follow as possible.

There are photocopiables to supplement many of the activities.

Preparation

Music Express is designed to minimise your preparation time.

Look out for the icons next to the activity headings which indicate things you need to prepare.

Key to icons

 Photocopiable icon: some activities require photocopies or activity cards to be made from a particular photocopiable.

 CD icon: you will need to have access to a CD player for an activity.

 Videoclip and picture icons: you will need to have access to a computer for an activity to show videoclips and pictures on the CD-ROM. (You might like to use a computer-compatible projector to show the videoclips and pictures on a screen for the whole class to see more easily.)

 Music icons: sheet music for the associated song is found on the CD-ROM.

Other resources

Classroom percussion

You will need to have a range of classroom percussion instruments available.

Many activities suggest that several members of the class play instruments at the same time. If necessary, pupils can share instruments and take turns to play.

Specific activities recommend the instruments you will need, but you should use the instruments that you have available.

For a class of 30 pupils, aim to have at least the following:

- Tuned percussion

  1 alto xylophone

  1 alto metallophone

  1 set of chime bars

  a selection of beaters

- A range of untuned percussion instruments, eg

  tambours

  drums

  wood blocks

cabassas

maracas

electronic keyboard (at least one)

- Other interesting soundmakers, eg

ocean drum

rainmaker

whistles

wind chimes

Instrumental lessons

Whenever appropriate, invite members of the class who are having instrumental lessons to bring their instruments into classroom music lessons.

If you are not sure which notes particular instruments use, ask the child's instrumental teacher.

Recording and evaluating

Recording on cassette or video

Have a cassette recorder and blank audio cassettes available during your music lessons. Recording pupils' work is important for monitoring their progress.

Children enjoy listening to their performances and contributing to the evaluation of their own and their classmates' work.

Many activities include movement as well as music. If you have a video camera available, video the performance. If not, invite members of your class or another class to watch and offer feedback.

Help for teachers

Teaching tips and background information

These are provided throughout next to the activity or activities to which they refer.

Dance and movement

Encourage movement in activities wherever appropriate as well as when specifically mentioned - it is an important means of musical learning.

Group work

The activities suggest appropriate group sizes. Be flexible, especially if your class has little or no experience of group work. Group work may be introduced into classroom music lessons gradually. Those activities which suggest group work may also be managed as whole class activities.

Teaching songs

We hope that teachers will lead the singing with their own voice, particularly with younger children. But in all instances we have assumed that the teacher will use the CD.

If you feel confident, teach yourself a song using the CD and then teach it to the children.

To rehearse songs with your class without the CD, you might:

- sing the melody without the words, to lah or dee;
- chant the rhythm of the words;
- sing the song line by line for the children to copy.

Teachers' videoclips

There are fifteen videoclips on the CD-ROM that demonstrate useful teaching techniques to use in class music lessons.

Clip	Contents
T 1	The song - Nanuma
T 2	Teaching a song line by line
T 3	Starting together: speed and starting note
T 4	Pitching the starting note
T 5	Discussing phrases
T 6	Clapping the rhythm of a phrase
T 7	Demonstrating pitch with hand
T 8	Internalising
T 9	Teaching a round
T 10	Playing by ear
T 11	Teaching an accompaniment
T 12	Singing a round in two parts
T 13	Discussing performance techniques
T 14	The performance
T 15	Appraising

Ongoing skills

'Ongoing skills' are identified by the QCA scheme of work as those skills which need to be continually developed and revisited. This is in addition to the activities in the six units. The QCA suggests that learning may take place as the opportunity arises throughout the school week, eg in short 5-minute sessions.

Music Express does not include a separate Ongoing skills unit, but addresses the skills throughout its activities. When using *Music Express* as a scheme, you will be fulfilling the learning objectives and outcomes of the QCA Ongoing skills unit.

If you teach music in one weekly lesson, as opposed to three shorter lessons, you may like to select activities from *Music Express* for supplementary 5-minute activities. By doing this, you will reinforce more regularly the development of the musical skills identified by the QCA.

Extension and future learning

A & C Black website

Music Express provides all the resources you will need for teaching a year of music. We hope, however, that you will use other songs and activities to ring the changes in subsequent years or to link with other National Curriculum subjects.

The website www.acblack.com/musicexpress lists the *Music Express* activities that were drawn from or inspired by other A & C Black books, and links to other books that will supplement the activities in *Music Express*.

GNOSSIENNE NO. 3

1 Listen to the melodies in *Gnossienne No 3*

- Listen to the extract of *Gnossienne No 3* (track 1) and invite the children to give their impressions of the piece.

- Ask the children if they recognise any of the solo instruments. (*Harp, flute and oboe.*)

- Listen to track 2 (*which identifies the solo instruments*) and ask the children to notice the melodies. (*They consist of short, repeated notes or of smooth rising and falling waves.*)

- Ask them to follow the *Gnossienne chart* on copies of the *Satie's scales* photocopiable as they listen to the music again.

Background information

- *Gnossienne No 3* is a set of piano pieces (here arranged for orchestra) by the French composer Satie (1866-1925). They are dances inspired by the ancient worlds of Greece and Knossos.

Teaching tips

- There are many different scales used throughout the world. They form the basis of melodies and chords.

- Chord - three or more notes played at the same time.

3 Perform invented chords

- Invite an individual to play a drone by alternating low and high A on tuned percussion, as on track 4: A A' A A' A A'...

  In the groups from activity 2, take turns to play the new chords from scale 1 over the drone. (*Play on the first of every four beats as in track 4. Direct when the groups should start and stop allowing enough time for each chord to become established but not boring.*) When all the groups have played their chords the drone fades to end the performance.

- Repeat the activity for the chords based on scale 2, this time playing a drone on D D' D D' D D'...

- Repeat for the chords based on scale 3, playing a drone on E E' E E' E E'...

- Discuss the effects which were achieved, if necessary, repeating the activity.

- As a class, choose four favourite chords from the scales (*two from one of the scales*). Appoint four individuals to play the alternating patterns for each chord, and four small groups to play a chord each.

- Perform the chords in any order and discuss the result. Try out a new order and keep experimenting until the class is satisfied with the result, eg

2 Explore scales used in *Gnossienne No 3* and invent chords

- Explain that in *Gnossienne No 3*, Satie builds the music out of three different sets of notes - three different scales.

- Listen to track 3 to hear Satie's three scales and the melodies he makes out of them.

- Invite individuals to demonstrate the scales using the *Satie's scales* photocopiable and tuned percussion or keyboard.

- Explain that Satie accompanies the melodies with chords played by other instruments. Show the children the chords on the *Satie's scales* photocopiable and invite volunteers to join in playing the chords with track 4 (*this track names each chord and plays it repeatedly over a drone bass*).

- Invite individuals to make a new chord from each scale (*eg C E F♯ from scale 1, or A B F from scale 2*). Ask the class to describe the sound produced (*eg tense, harsh, comfortable, sad, relaxed ...*).

- Divide the class into groups, and give each a keyboard or tuned percussion notes for each scale. The groups explore playing different combinations of notes from each scale. They then write down their favourite new chords in the space on the photocopiable and keep it for activity 3.

Teaching tips

- Appoint a conductor to direct the groups so that the transition from one chord to another is smooth.

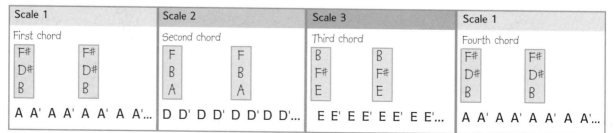

Scale 1	Scale 2	Scale 3	Scale 1
First chord	Second chord	Third chord	Fourth chord
F♯ F♯ D♯ D♯ B B	F F B B A A	B B F♯ F♯ E E	F♯ F♯ D♯ D♯ B B
A A' A A' A A' A A'...	D D' D D' D D' D D'...	E E' E E' E E' E E'...	A A' A A' A A' A A'...

- As a class, discuss what the children have learned about scales and chords.

Satie's scales

Gnossienne chart

Scale 1		Scale 2		Scale 3			
harp: repeated note melody	flute and harp: repeated note melody	oboe: repeated note melody	oboe: waves	harp: repeated note melody	flute and harp: repeated note melody	oboe: waves	flute: waves

Scale 1:

B♭ C D♯ E F♯ A

Satie's chord

A♭ C E

Scale 2:

G♯♭ A♭ B♭ D F

Satie's chord

D♭♭ F♭ A

Scale 3:

E♭ F♯ G♭ A♯♭ B♭ C♯ E

Satie's chord

E♭ G♭ B♭

Our chord from: Scale 1

Our chord from: Scale 2

Our chord from: Scale 3

Scales: sets of notes that we use to create melodies and chords

Chord: three or more notes played at the same time

Music Express Year 6 © A & C Black 2003
www.acblack.com/musicexpress

9

RELAY RACE

1 Compare and learn two chordal accompaniments for the song *Relay race*

- Listen to *Relay race* (track 5) which is sung in unison twice through, the second time with a different ending (*'yes we are'* is sung instead of *'keep on running'*). Ask the children to describe what happens in the piano accompaniment:

  - *the first time the song is sung, the accompaniment pattern stays the same; one chord is repeatedly played on the strong beat;*

  - *the second time, the accompaniment pattern changes; the chords change;*

  - *a fast bass drone, alternating between two notes is played throughout.*

- Show the children an enlarged copy of the *Relay accompaniments* photocopiable and as a class follow the accompaniments as you listen to track 5 again. (*Each is played four times.*)

- Ask which accompaniment the children prefer and why. (*Some may prefer the single chord because it gives a feeling of relaxed steadiness, others may like the tension which the changing chords give to the song.*)

- Use the *Relay accompaniments* photocopiable to learn the accompaniments on tuned percussion, on keyboards or on guitar. (*Remember to play the accompaniment four times through for each repetition of the song.*)

Teaching tips

- Unison - all performers performing the same thing at the same time.

- Explain that the choice of which accompaniment is better comes down to personal preference.

- The note which names a chord is its bass note. The rest of the chord name tells you what other notes the chord contains, eg D major contains the notes D (bass note), F#, and A. The three chords used in *Relay race* are D major, G major, and A minor 7.

- Attempt whichever accompaniment your class can manage and for which you have instrumental resources.

3 Perform *Relay race* with the chordal accompaniment

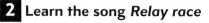

- Having practised *Relay race* in sections and ensured that the words and melody are accurately learned, rehearse the song with one of the chord accompaniments. Invite a small group to play while the others sing. Use track 5 as backing support if you wish, and check that:

  - the singing remains clear and well-controlled;

  - the words are pronounced clearly and not rushed, particularly the beginnings and ends of words;

  - the children are singing the melody of the song accurately.

2 Learn the song *Relay race*

- Write the words of the song *Relay race* on the board and teach it using the CD. The song is in four sections (tracks 6–9), and is sung twice, the second time with a different ending (track 10). Listen carefully then sing each section separately:

1 Look at me, I'm lightning, I am speedy, I am frightening, I'm the leader of the pack, I'm tearing down the track to pass the baton on.

2 (on.) Go! Go! Go! Go! This is a relay race! No time to be slow!

3 See the crowd are on their feet, They loudly clap and cheer: hooray,

4 For we are the fastest! We are the winners! We are the champions! Keep on running! (*Second time*) Yes we are!

- Practise adding the hand claps in section 4, tracks 8 and 9:

1	+	2	+	3	+	4
					👏	👏
We	are		the	fast	-	est,

Relay accompaniments

Accompaniment 1:

1	+	2	+	3	+	4	+	1	+	2	+	3	+	4	+
A F# D								A F# D							
D	D'	D	D'	D	D'	D	D'	D	D'	D	D'	D	D'	D	D'

A F# D								A F# D							
D	D'	D	D'	D	D'	D	D'	D	D'	D	D'	D	D'	D	D'

Accompaniment 2:

1	+	2	+	3	+	4	+	1	+	2	+	3	+	4	+
A F# D				B G D		A F# D		A F# D				B G D		A F# D	
D	D'	D	D'	D	D'	D	D'	D	D'	D	D'	D	D'	D	D'

A F# D				B G D		A F# D		C A E		B G D				A F# D	
D	D'	D	D'	D	D'	D	D'	D	D'	D	D'	D	D'	D	D'

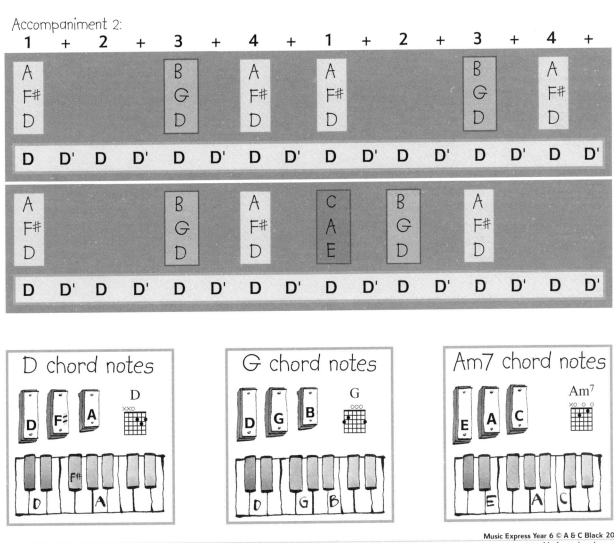

D chord notes	G chord notes	Am7 chord notes
D F# A D	D G B G	E A C Am7
D F# A	D G B	E A C

A ROUND RELAY

1 Perform *Relay race* as a four-part round

- Revise singing *Relay race* using track 5 if required.
- Listen to track 11, and ask how the song is organised.
  (Relay race, which is a four-part round, is performed twice through by four voices.)

  Ask when the entry points occur.
  (At the beginning of each section, on the words 'on', 'see' and 'for'.)
- Practise singing the song as a round in two groups, then three, then four.

Teaching tips

- A round is a piece of music in which two or more performers or groups start one after the other. As each performer reaches the end of the music, they start again – the music going round and round – hence the name.
- Entry points are those points in a round when the next performer may begin. Rounds may have two or more entry points, making them two-part, three-part, four-part, or more. But any round may be performed by as few as two performers.

Teaching tips

- Appoint a conductor to tap or signal the beat to help everyone keep in time and to prevent the song from speeding up or slowing down.
- It may help to chant the words as a round first so that everyone understands how the rhythm of each part fits together.
- Make sure there are confident singers in each group and that the groups are secure singing on their own.
- It may take several practices to be able to perform the round all the way through in four parts.
- Encourage each group to be aware of the other parts whilst singing their own.

2 Add the accompaniment to *Relay race*

- Divide the class into five groups, one to accompany the others singing *Relay race* as a round.
  (The accompaniment group keeps repeating their part until group four sings the ending 'Yes we are'.)
- Rehearse the round with the accompaniment several times. Check that:
  - each group performs the hand claps together at the same time;
  - all the parts are well-balanced in volume - no group dominating the others;
  - the song is sung musically and with enjoyment.

3 Evaluate a performance of *Relay race*

- Record a performance of *Relay race* as rehearsed in activity 2.
- Listen back, and appraise the performance as a class. Consider ways to improve, eg:
  - would adding any other accompaniment instruments enrich the song or crowd it?
  - does the chosen accompaniment work well?
  - would a different speed be more suitable?
  - how could the performance capture the spirit of the song more?
- Perform the song again. Try swapping groups to give everyone the opportunity to perform the accompaniment and sing in a different order in the round.

NANUMA

1 Learn to sing *Nanuma* and play an ostinato 🔊 12-13))

- Listen to *Nanuma* (track 12). Ask how many musical phrases the song has. *(There are four phrases. Each line of the song is a phrase.)*

  Ask what the four phrases have in common and what is different about each.
  (The phrases have the same words and the same rhythm. The first and last phrase are exactly the same, but each of the other phrases starts on a higher note each time.)

- Teach the song using track 13 *(this track leaves a gap after each phrase for the children to copy).*

  1 Nanuma wyaeh, Nanuma.
  2 Nanuma wyaeh, Nanuma.
  3 Nanuma wyaeh, Nanuma.
  4 Nanuma wyaeh, Nanuma.

  All trace the pitch movement with hands as you learn the song and concentrate on being able to pitch the notes accurately.

- Ask the children to notice the ostinato part played on xylophone as they listen to track 12 again. When the track ends, ask volunteers to sing (to *la*) the ostinato part then play it.

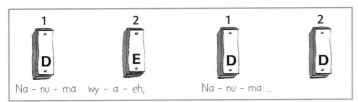

Teaching tips

Nanuma is demonstrated in the extra teaching videoclips on the CD-ROM:

- T1 – T15

- Use any available melody instruments to play the *Nanuma* phrases, eg recorders, or instruments from home.

2 Explore the harmony in *Nanuma* 📄 p14 🔊 14))

- Divide the class into four groups, and allocate each group a phrase of the song.

  The first group sings the first phrase over and over as an ostinato. When this is established, the second group joins in singing their phrase as an ostinato. Then the third and fourth groups join in in the same way.
  (This activity is recorded on track 14 if the children need support.)

  As you sing, all listen to the effect. Explain that you are singing in harmony.
  (Harmony is created when notes are sung or played at the same time.)

- Each group works out the melody of their phrase by ear using tuned percussion or keyboards *(notes D E F F♯ A B C')*. Each group writes the notes of their melody in the space on the *Nanuma phrases* photocopiable.
  (A completed answer sheet is provided on the CD-ROM.)

- Build the harmony on tuned percussion as before: the first group perform their melody on tuned percussion as an ostinato and the other three groups join in in turn.

Background information

- *Nanuma* is a traditional African song.
- Harmony is used to describe any number of changing layers of sound, sung or played at the same time. A chord has a more specific definition used to describe three or more notes played at the same time.

3 Sing *Nanuma* as a round 🔊 15))

- Listen to track 15 and ask how the song is performed.
  (It is sung once through in unison and then twice through as a four-part round.)

- Divide the class into four groups to practise singing the song as a round with track 15.

  When everyone is confident, practise without the CD – invite individuals to provide support by adding the xylophone accompaniment from activity 1.

- Record a performance of the class singing *Nanuma* as a round, then listen back and discuss:

  – whether the class could hear the harmony build as each part entered in turn;

  – whether each part entered clearly and confidently.

Nanuma phrases

Phrase 1

1				2		1			2

D

Na – nu – ma   wy – a – eh,   Na – nu – ma,

Phrase 2

1				2		1			2

Na – nu – ma   wy – a – eh,   Na – nu – ma,

Phrase 3

1				2		1			2

Na – nu – ma   wy – a – eh,   Na – nu – ma,

Phrase 4

1				2		1			2

Na – nu – ma   wy – a – eh,   Na – nu – ma,

Music Express Year 6 © A & C Black 2003
www.acblack.com/musicexpress

AROUND NANUMA

1 Learn to sing an ostinato accompaniment to *Nanuma*

- Revise singing ***Nanuma*** as a four-part round *(track 15)*.

- Listen to the phrase on track 16 and ask how it differs from the other song phrases.
  (Although the rhythm is the same, the melodic shape is different. Instead of going up then back down to the starting note, the melody goes down then back up to the starting note.)

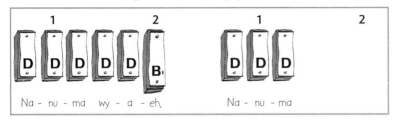

- Invite an individual to play the phrase on a tuned instrument; the others join in singing it.

- Play track 15 and all quietly sing the new phrase as an ostinato accompaniment. If possible, record a performance and listen back to discuss how effective it is.

2 Add a two-chord accompaniment to *Nanuma*

- Teach the class the following chords which they may perform on tuned percussion, keyboards or guitar:

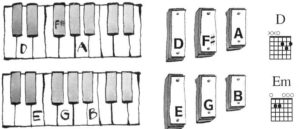

- Listen to a performance of the chords as an accompaniment to ***Nanuma*** *(track 17)*, then invite members of the class to take turns joining in with the CD to accompany the song.
  (Encourage the children to feel when the chord changes, noticing that it changes in the same place in each phrase.)

- All sing the song in unison, and take turns performing the chord accompaniment.

3 Decide on a structure for a performance of *Nanuma* and perform to a friendly audience

- Ask the class to decide how you will combine some or all of the elements you have learnt to make a performance of the song, starting by considering how best to begin and end the performance. Write the options on the board for the class to decide, eg:

  – introduction: begin and end with the tuned percussion ostinato (from Lesson 4 activity 1);

  – sing the song in unison;

  – sing the song in unison with the tuned percussion ostinato;

  – sing the song as a four-part round;

  – play the phrases of the song on melody instruments;

  – accompany with the sung ostinato (from activity 1);

  – accompany with the two-chord accompaniment.

- When you have decided upon an order, rehearse the song and when confident perform to a friendly audience.

Teaching tips

- The chord sequence is the same for each phrase, and follows the xylophone accompaniment from lesson 4 activity 1.

- Sing the song several times to let several children take part in accompanying and feeling where the chord changes.

JUNKANOO

1 Learn the four-part round, *Junkanoo*

• Teach *Junkanoo* in unison using track 18.

1 We've got a bell, we've got a drum,
   Junkanoo has begun.
2 Feel that Gombay beat,
   Giving life to your dancing feet.
3 Ev'rybody's on holiday,
   We'll dance the night away.
4 Now you know it's Junkanoo,
   Come on, let's go!

• Listen to track 19 to hear *Junkanoo* performed as a four-part round. Practise singing *Junkanoo* as a round in two parts and then four parts.

Background information

• *Junkanoo* is a Jamaican festivity, in which processions of masked dancers, drummers and fife players sing and play through the streets.

2 Rehearse the performance of *Junkanoo*

• Perform *Junkanoo* as a four-part round and all mark the steady beat by tapping fingertips on knees or clapping quietly.

• Teach groups of children the accompaniments on the *Junkanoo ideas* photocopiable.

• Using the skills and knowledge learnt from this unit, decide as a class how you will fit these parts together to make your version of *Junkanoo* (*eg start with a percussion introduction, add other accompaniment ideas, add unison voices, continue as a two- or four-part round*).

Decide whether you will use track 19 for backing support, then rehearse your version of the song.
(*Can someone in the class suggest a really good way of ending the piece?*)

• Discuss ways to improve your performance, eg

  – is the singing expressive?

  – is it enjoyable to listen to?

  – is everyone in time with each other?

  – does the song start and finish confidently?

  – could the song be performed as a procession with dance moves?

3 Perform *Junkanoo* to a friendly audience and assess the effect on the performers

• When you are ready, perform your version of the song to a friendly audience. Afterwards discuss the children's reactions to the experience. How did performing to an audience affect the way they sang and played, eg

  – were they nervous, excited?

  – more, or less able to concentrate?

  – more, or less able to listen to each other and work together?

• Ask the class to suggest how their performance might be improved in the light of their experience. (*Some children's ability to perform well will have been affected by nervousness, while others may have been happy and excited but unfocussed. Good preparation through concentrated rehearsal will help both.*)

Teaching tips

• The singing needs to be strong without shouting.

• Do not always sit down to rehearse; spend some time standing up.

• Write your agreed structure on the board where everyone can see it.

• To help the children reach the high notes when they are singing, encourage them to think high.

Junkanoo ideas

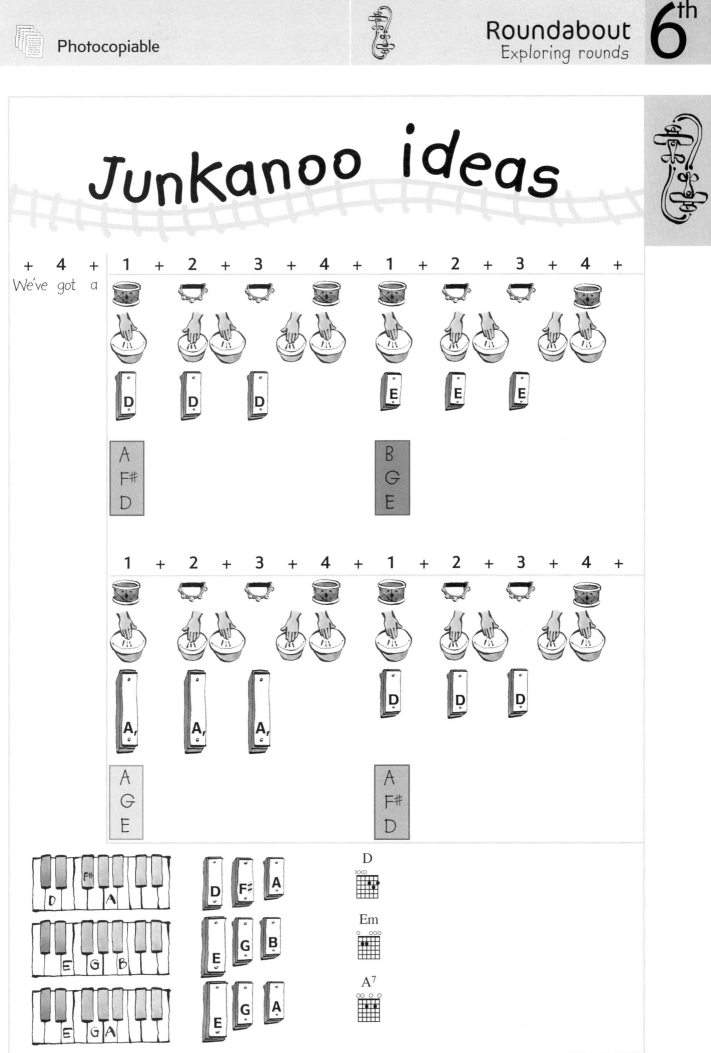

LOOPY WEATHER

1 Listen to *Loopy weather* and discuss how the piece was composed 🔊 20))

- Listen to *Loopy weather*, and ask the children to identify the sounds they hear.
  (There are spoken phrases accompanied by repeating patterns played on drums and synthesiser.)

- Explain that the composer recorded the following phrases from weather bulletins as a theme for this composition and altered them using an effects processor and an equaliser:
  - *'the weather forecast'*;
  - *'basically a settled pattern'*;
  - *'but it depends on the cyclone'*;
  - *'a chilly start in the north west'*;
  - *'but occasionally cloudy'*.

  Listen again to track 20 and ask these questions:
  - which of the phrases occurs first? (*'The weather forecast'.*)
  - how many times does the phrase *'basically a settled pattern'* occur? *(Twelve times)*

  Explain that the phrase *'basically a settled pattern'* has been 'looped'.

Background information

- A sampler is capable of recording sounds and altering them by making them higher/lower, playing them forwards/backwards, or cutting them into sections.

- Sending a sound through an effects processor can make it sound as though in a small room or a large resonant hall.

- An equaliser (EQ) can change sound quality (*timbre*), eg make a sound bright/dull, thin, boomy ...

- Loop - a sound or pattern of sounds repeated over and over by means of an electronic device.

Teaching tips
- You may need to listen to the tracks several times to find the answers to the questions.

3 Copy the processed vocal phrases and perform them with the recording of *Loopy weather* 📄 p19 🔊 20-21))

- Divide the class into five groups and allocate one spoken phrase from *Loopy weather* to each group.

- Each group practises reproducing the processed sound of their given phrase with their voices using track 21 if necessary.

- Listen again to track 20, all following the piece on the *Processed weather* photocopiable. Each group listens carefully for when their phrase occurs.

- Perform *Loopy weather* with track 20, each group joining in with their processed phrase as it occurs.

- As a class, discuss which of the processed phrases were easy to reproduce and which were harder.

2 Listen to the processed phrases in *Loopy weather* 🔊 20-22))

- Listen to *Loopy weather* again *(track 20)*. Demonstrate how each spoken phrase has been altered by a sampler or sound processor by listening to the original phrase followed by its processed sound *(track 21)*.

  Ask which two phrases have some syllables repeated rhythmically. *('The weather forecast' and 'a chilly start in the north west'.)*

  Listen to track 21 again, and discuss how each phrase has been altered:
  - *'the weather forecast'* - has echo *(delay)* added to it;
  - *'basically a settled pattern'* - has been made to sound thinner;
  - *'but it depends on the cyclone'* - has been slowed down and made lower in pitch;
  - *'a chilly start in the north west'* - has been speeded up and made higher in pitch;
  - *'but occasionally cloudy'* - has been reversed *(in track 20 it is played backwards then forwards)*.

- Listen to a triangle sound followed by its processed sound *(track 22)* and ask which of the above processes has been applied to it. *(It has been reversed.)*

  Listen again to track 20 to hear where the triangle processed sound occurs in *Loopy weather*. *(It first occurs just before the phrase 'basically a settled pattern' starts.)*

- Click on the relevant links on the *Music Express* website to give the children the opportunity to explore more sounds played forwards and backwards.

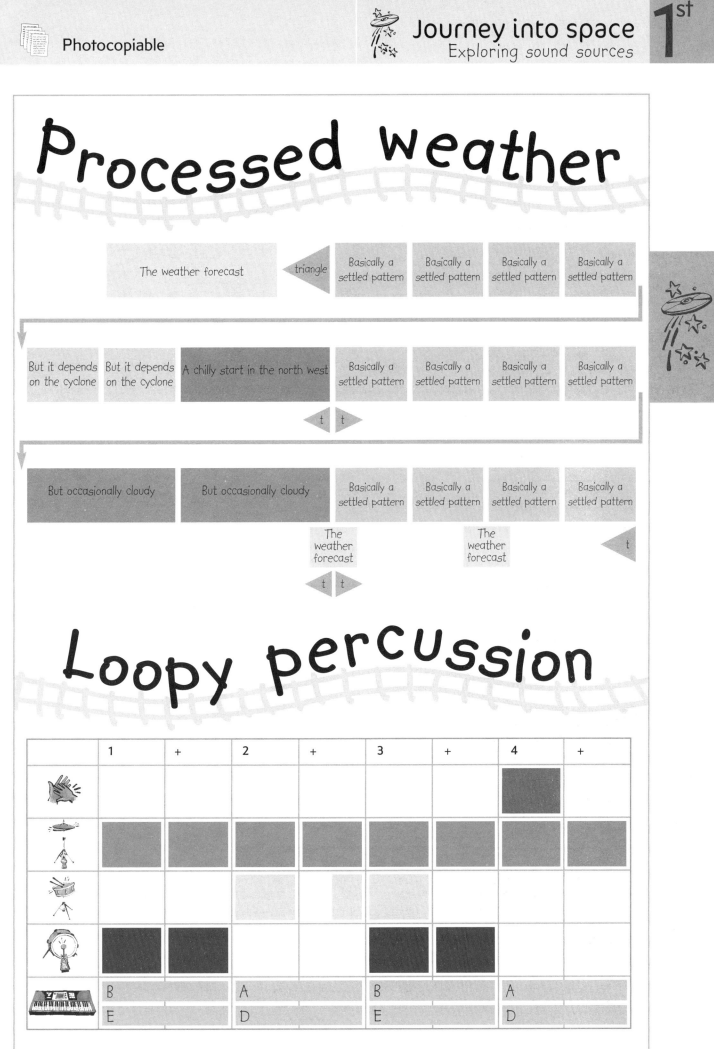

Processed weather

| | | The weather forecast | triangle | Basically a settled pattern | Basically a settled pattern | Basically a settled pattern | Basically a settled pattern |

But it depends on the cyclone | But it depends on the cyclone | A chilly start in the north west | Basically a settled pattern | Basically a settled pattern | Basically a settled pattern | Basically a settled pattern

t t

But occasionally cloudy | But occasionally cloudy | Basically a settled pattern | Basically a settled pattern | Basically a settled pattern | Basically a settled pattern

The weather forecast | The weather forecast | t

t t

Loopy percussion

	1	+	2	+	3	+	4	+
👏							▦	
🔔	▦	▦	▦	▦	▦	▦	▦	▦
🥁			▦	▦				
🥁	▦	▦			▦	▦		
🎹	B / E		A / D		B / E		A / D	

EXPLORING LOOPS

1 **Revise the different processes applied to spoken phrases in *Loopy weather***

- Listen again to *Loopy weather* (track 20) and ask the children to remember how the phrases in the composition had been processed. *(See lesson 1, activity 2.)*

- Explain that track 23 uses the same five phrases but this time they have been processed differently. Write the following questions on the board and ask the children to work out the answers as they listen to the track:

  - which phrase has been speeded up and made higher in pitch? *('basically a settled pattern')*
  - which phrase has been slowed down and made lower in pitch? *('the weather forecast')*
  - which phrase has had echo added to it? *('but occasionally cloudy')*
  - which phrase has been made to sound thinner? *('but it depends on the cyclone')*
  - which phrase has been reversed? *('a chilly start in the north west')*

2 **Learn a simplified percussion loop accompaniment for *Loopy weather***

- Listen to the simplified accompaniment to *Loopy weather* on track 24, all following it on the *Loopy percussion* photocopiable. *Each instrument is added one after the other in the order: hi-hat (cymbals), bass drum, snare drum, clap, keyboard).*

  Explain that the composer invented rhythm patterns for the instruments which are performed together as a loop.

- Teach each of the patterns to the class, using these or similar instruments, then divide the class into five groups, one for each pattern. Each group begin performing their pattern in the order on the CD and continues the complete loop for several repetitions (you may like to use track 24 again for support).

- When the class can perform the loop confidently, try it without the CD *(the hi-hat group will be responsible for maintaining a clear and steady beat).*

- Click on the relevant links from the *Music express* website to give the children the opportunity to create their own loops on a computer. *(There are several different links available for the children to explore.)*

3 **Invent spoken phrases on a chosen theme to process and perform with a percussion loop accompaniment**

- Divide the class into small groups. Each group writes a list of five or six short phrases on a chosen theme *(eg traffic report, football commentary, news item...).* They then practise saying the phrases in the following processed ways:

  - speak slow and low;
  - speak fast and high;
  - make an echo effect;
  - alter the tone of the voice by whispering, speaking into a tin can, using a microphone ...
  - speak the phrase backwards *(encourage the children to copy the mouth shapes and tongue movements in reverse).*

- Each group chooses their favourite processed way to say their phrases and decides on an order to perform them over the percussion loop *(track 24).* *(One processed phrase might be repeated rhythmically as a loop throughout, as with 'basically a settled pattern' in **Loopy weather**.)*

- Each group rehearses their processed phrases with the backing track *(track 24)* and then performs to the class.

Teaching tips

- Your school keyboards or computers may have the ability to sample and process sounds. If so, encourage the children to use this equipment to process their phrases.

- Instead of using the backing track, encourage the rest of the class to accompany each group with the loop practised in activity 2, or one of the children's own loops invented on the computer.

- If a drum machine is available, encourage individuals to programme the accompaniment patterns into it.

ELECTRONIC SOUNDS

1 Explore an electronic keyboard to recreate the sounds used in *Alpha*  25-26))

- Listen to *Alpha* (track 25), and ask what happens to the music overall. (*It builds both in volume and number of sounds playing.*)

  Ask what the children think the music could be describing (*eg the emergence of a space creature from an egg, sunrise, something getting gradually closer ...*).

- Listen to track 26 which demonstrates the melody played on keyboard, then listen again to track 25, following the melody throughout. Ask the children:

  – how many times the melody is played (*six times*);

  – whether the melody is played on the same keyboard sound throughout. (*No, it changes on the penultimate repetition.*)

- Invite a volunteer to explore the sounds on your keyboard (*use the notes F E and D from the opening of the Alpha melody*).

  Ask the class to identify which sounds most closely match the sounds used for the melody on track 25 (*eg clarinet then brass sounds*).

- Listen again to the beginning of track 25, but this time focus on the accompaniment. Invite a volunteer to match the sound on a keyboard as before, this time playing the notes D A D' A (*eg an oboe sound*).

- Ask the children whether they heard any of the processing effects examined in weeks 1 and 2 in this extract of *Alpha*. (*Yes, echo effects - delay - are used throughout.*)

Teaching tips

- There is no correct answer to what *Alpha* is describing. Encourage the children to explore their imaginations.

- Encourage individuals to work out the entire melody of *Alpha* by ear.

- All keyboard sounds vary. The suggestions here are approximations.

Background information

- *Alpha* was written by the Greek composer Vangelis (born 1943), who composes film music using computers and electronics. He is particularly known for the film music to *Chariots of fire*.

- A synthesiser is an electronic device, often with a keyboard, that can generate and manipulate sounds (eg change dynamics, add delay).

- A keyboard is like a synthesiser but in general the sounds are fixed.

- A sound module is a synthesiser without a keyboard.

2 Compose a melody and arrange it for an electronic keyboard

- Explain that the class is going to compose a piece which, like *Alpha*, builds both in volume and number of sounds playing.

- Invite a confident individual to improvise a simple melody to repeat six times on a keyboard using only the notes D E F and G.

- As a class, discuss which keyboard sound would be suitable for the quiet beginning (*the first two repetitions of the melody*). All join in humming the melody quietly as it is played.

  Next, decide on a suitable sound for the middle two repetitions of the melody which clearly suggest getting bigger or closer. All join in singing moderately loudly to 'ah'.

  For the final two repetitions of the melody, find a bold, strong sound and all join in singing loudly to 'lah'.

- Invite individuals to suggest accompaniment ideas to introduce with each repetition, eg drum beat, sustained background sounds, repeating bass pattern on a xylophone, vocal or instrumental sound effects ... (*If you have them, use as many keyboards as possible in this composition.*)

3 Perform and appraise the class keyboard composition

- Rehearse the class composition.

- Record a performance of the class composition, then listen back to discuss:

  – how well the composition implied something building or growing;

  – whether the melody, performed on keyboard and voices, built in strength;

  – whether the accompaniment ideas were added effectively;

  – whether the accompaniment ideas made full use of dynamic contrast.

IN THE SEQUENCER

1 Learn about sequencers by following a score of *Crazy green bottles*

- Listen to *Crazy green bottles* (*track 27*), without revealing the title of the piece of music, and ask the children to identify which well-known tune has been adapted for this piece.
  (*Ten green bottles.*)

- Explain that *Crazy green bottles* was composed on a computer using a sequencer. Show the children the score on the *Sequenced sounds* photocopiable and explain that it represents a window of the sequencer. Ask the children to describe the visual representation of the music, eg:

  - each layer (1–10) represents a different sound or group of sounds;

  - each block (from left to right) shows the start and end points of a musical idea;

  - the time line at the top (1–53) shows even units of time moving from left to right;

  - each count on the time line (*ten counts are spoken aloud at the beginning of the track*) is equal to one group of four beats.

  Ask which count the first bottle melody starts and ends on. (*It starts on count 13 and finishes on count 21.*)

  Explain that the percussion 1 part (*layer 7*) is looped (*repeated without a gap*). Ask how many counts the loop lasts. (*Four counts.*)

- All watch videoclip 1 to follow the same piece of music live on a computer monitor. Notice that the cursor line shows the progress of the music. Next, watch videoclip 2 which demonstrates individual layers.

Teaching tips
- You will need to play the CD track to the class several times for them to work out where to play their rhythm patterns.
- The children will need to perform their rhythm at the speed given on track 27 so that it is in time with *Crazy green bottles*.

3 Add a rhythm pattern layer on the *Sequenced sounds* photocopiable

- Divide the class into groups of three or four, each with a copy of the *Sequenced sounds* photocopiable. Practise clapping the rhythms shown at the bottom of the photocopiable with track 28.

  Each group chooses one of the rhythm patterns to clap during the track. They should decide which counts they will perform their pattern on, and draw a block for each time it is played.

- Each group practises clapping their rhythm patterns at the chosen places in the track.

- Each group performs their rhythm patterns with the CD track.
  (*To help the groups know when to play, ask the class to count aloud throughout.*)

- Invite a volunteer from each group to transfer their rhythm pattern onto untuned percussion or keyboard drum sounds and perform with the CD.

  Invite several children to perform at the same time with the CD and discuss as a class which rhythms work well together.

Background information
- A sequencer is a piece of software that enables a composer to organise (layer and sequence) sounds in a composition. It enables composers to record and control the information from several synthesisers, sound processors, samplers and effects units. For most composers it is the heart of the music studio, providing a tool to realise instantly their musical ideas.

2 Follow the rhythm of the melody in *Crazy green bottles*

- Listen again to *Crazy green bottles*, following the bottle melody (*layer 2*) on the *Sequenced sounds* photocopiable. Ask how many times the melody is repeated (*four*), and what is different about the third and fourth repetitions. (*They are performed at double speed.*)

- All clap the rhythm of the first two repetitions of the melody with track 27, and when confident at this speed, attempt clapping the rhythm at double speed.
  (*It is physically very challenging and very difficult to get the rhythm precise at this speed.*)

  Explain that the composer recorded the melody at the steady speed and used the computer to speed it up. This is one of the benefits of using a computer sequencer.

  All watch videoclip 3 which shows what the melody looks like at normal and double speed in a different window in the sequencer.

- Ask the children to suggest other benefits of composing using computer software, eg

  - to be able to edit and correct performances in a similar way to editing and correcting text in a word processor;

  - to be able to hear the entire piece emerging and assess its effectiveness.

Photocopiable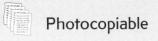

Journey into space
Exploring sound sources
4th

Sequenced sounds

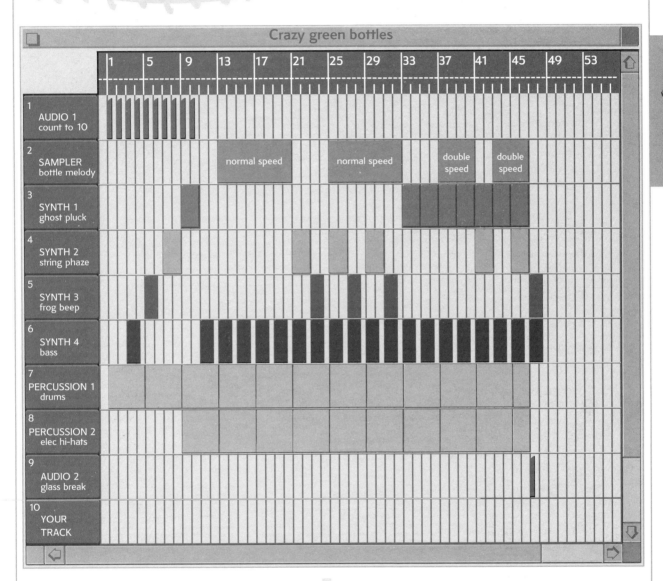

Crazy green bottles

	1	5	9	13	17	21	25	29	33	37	41	45	49	53

1 AUDIO 1 count to 10

2 SAMPLER bottle melody — normal speed, normal speed, double speed, double speed

3 SYNTH 1 ghost pluck

4 SYNTH 2 string phaze

5 SYNTH 3 frog beep

6 SYNTH 4 bass

7 PERCUSSION 1 drums

8 PERCUSSION 2 elec hi-hats

9 AUDIO 2 glass break

10 YOUR TRACK

Rhythm patterns

Each of these rhythm patterns lasts one count of four beats.

Choose one of the rhythm patterns to perform as an extra layer in 'Crazy green bottles'.

Shade in the blocks on track 10 above (your track) to show when to play your chosen rhythm.

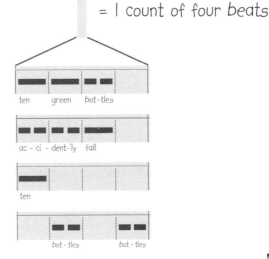

= 1 count of four beats

ten   green   bot-tles

ac - ci - dent-'ly fall

ten

bot - tles   bot - tles

Music Express Year 6 © A & C Black 2003
www.acblack.com/musicexpress

23

SOUNDS OF THE FUTURE

1 **Discuss suitable instruments and electronic equipment for a class futuristic composition, *Loop to the future***

- In advance, allocate an area of the classroom for each piece of equipment and its purposes as listed below. Explain that the class is going to compose a futuristic piece of music called *Loop to the future* which will be organised in layers as in a sequencer. In groups of four, the children will visit each area in turn. Their task will be to use the equipment to find musical ideas for each of the layers:

1	– Layer 1: computer software or drum machine for exploring drum patterns and loops – these might use software and website links *(see lesson 2)*;
2	– Layer 2: an electronic keyboard for inventing a futuristic-sounding melody *(see lesson 3)*;
3	– Layer 3: another keyboard or computer for finding sound effects *(these might use software or website links)*;
4	– Layer 4: a microphone and amplifier or karaoke machine to explore vocal sounds *(see lesson 1)*;
5	– Layer 5: a xylophone/metallophone for exploring melodic ostinati *(see lesson 3)*;
6	– Layer 6: electronic equipment/gadgets such as a radio or digital watch for sound effects;
7	– Layer 7: untuned percussion for rhythm patterns;
8	– Layer 8: classroom objects and other sources of interesting sound effects.

Discuss the task for each different area and invite volunteers to demonstrate initial ideas to the class.

Explain that each group will need to remember their ideas from each area and so discuss ways of recording them *(eg using graphic notation, saving work on the computer, using an audio cassette to record sounds...).*

Teaching tips

- Encourage children to bring in instruments, electronic gadgets or other sources of sound effects from home.

- Remind the children of the effects they have created during the other lessons in the unit.

- It might be helpful to listen to some of the pieces of music from the unit again to remind the children of the effects used.

- When the children use electronic equipment such as keyboards or computer, they should remember to make a note of all the settings they have chosen.

- The *Loop to the future* composition may be completed by pairs or small groups using computer software alone, if available.

Teaching tips

- Encourage the children to be as imaginative and innovative as possible when creating their futuristic sounds. They should imagine what instruments might sound like in the future, and what the mood and atmosphere might be.

2 **Groups create a bank of futuristic sounds to use in their composition, *Loop to the future***

- Divide the class into groups and allocate each group an area to start in. Agree a period of time for exploring each area before moving on to the next.

- Stop the class at regular intervals for groups or individuals to demonstrate their sounds. Encourage the children to comment on each other's sounds and consider how futuristic they sound.

- Each group finds a way to write down and/or record their ideas from each area to remember at the next lesson.

3 **Groups share work in progress**

- Each group continues working in each area in turn, and sharing ideas with the class as they go.

LOOP TO THE FUTURE

1 Combine each group's sounds with the drum loop layer

- Set up as for the previous lesson, and make sure each group has the records of their musical ideas for each area. Have available a copy of the class *Loop to the future* score *(available to print out and enlarge from the CD-ROM).*

- Allocate each group to an area and allow them time to revise their ideas for that layer from last lesson *(see the list they were working from in Lesson 5 activity 1).*

  Each group chooses the most effective of their futuristic sounds to perform to the class.

- The group using the computer/drum machine plays their loop, and counts out the repetitions. Each count will represent one unit of time on the class score.

  The other groups think about how their melody, ostinato, vocal phrase, rhythm pattern or sound effect fits with the drum loop. *(They may choose to alter their ideas slightly to make them work well with the loop.)*

  Each group takes turns rehearsing in time with the loop.

Teaching tips

- Explain that the purpose of this activity is to find good combinations of pre-composed musical ideas through trial and error.

- Encourage all groups to revise their ideas as the piece develops.

- The *Loop to the future* score provides space for ten layers – one for each area, and a few extra if needed.

- This score may be photocopied and enlarged for use as a class score, or given to the children to fill in individually.

- If the class composition is longer than space allows on the score, two sheets may be joined.

- Always perform, revise and develop each group's idea before notating it.

2 Decide how to 'sequence' the class piece, *Loop to the future*

- The class start organising the layers into a piece of 'sequenced' music. As the class decides when each layer will be played, they fill in the blocks for it on the class score, eg

  - begin with Layer 1 – the drum loop, counting the repetitions as before and filling in the blocks on the score;

  - add Layer 2 – the keyboard melody, deciding as a class how many times to repeat it during the piece, and on which counts it will begin and end – fill in the blocks on the score.

- Listen to these layers performed together and decide as a class on which layers to add next, blocking them in on the score and trying out the results. *(Some sound effects may be repeated regularly, others played only once or sporadically.)*

  Each group completes their layer of the score when they are happy with the effect.

- Discuss the overall effect of the class piece, and how it might be improved, eg

  - did everyone keep in time with the loop?

  - did everyone manage to begin on the correct count, or would it be helpful for some children to direct their group by counting aloud throughout?

  - did it sound cluttered and if so which sounds might be played less often?

  - was there a suitable balance between all parts, eg were any too loud?

  - did it sound futuristic?

3 Play *Loop to the future* to a friendly audience

- Rehearse the class piece again, following the suggestions for improvement discussed in activity 2.

- When everyone is confident of their part, record the piece. Arrange for a friendly audience to listen to the recording of *Loop to the future*.

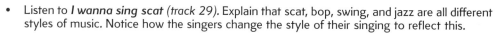
I WANNA SING SCAT

1 **Learn *I wanna sing scat* and discuss the relationship between the words and the music**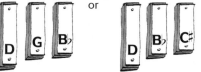

- Listen to *I wanna sing scat (track 29)*. Explain that scat, bop, swing, and jazz are all different styles of music. Notice how the singers change the style of their singing to reflect this.

- Teach both parts of the song by singing each in turn to track 29.

Part 1	Part 2
Vs 1 I wanna sing scat, sing scat, I wanna sing scat, sing scat, I wanna sing scat, sing scat, I wanna sing scat, sing scat, sing scat	Cool cat, cool cat, Cool cat, cool cat, Cool cat, cool cat, Cool cat, cool cat.
Vs 2 I wanna sing bop ...	Be bop ...
Vs 3 I wanna sing swing ...	Ring-a-ding ...
Vs 4 I wanna sing jazz ...	Jazza-ma-tazz ...
Vs 1 I wanna sing scat ...	Cool cat ...

> **Background information**
>
> • Scat, bop, and swing are all jazz singing styles made popular during the first half of the 20th century by the great names of jazz, including Dizzy Gillespie, Charlie Parker and Duke Ellington.

- When the parts are secure, divide the class in half to sing the parts together, initially with track 29 then with backing track 30.

- Ask what makes the two parts easy to learn.
  (*The words are repeated. Both parts have a repetitive rhythm and a strong steady beat. Part 2 is an ostinato – a short melodic phrase is repeated four times.*)

> **Teaching tips**
>
> - Ostinato – a short rhythmic or melodic phrase which is played repeatedly.
>
> - Those playing the second part on instruments should remember there is an introduction on the recording before the song begins.
>
> - When groups are composing their own ostinati for the song, give them as much time and space as possible to try out their ideas and rehearse them with track 31.

3 **Perform the song with the new ostinato parts**

- Each group takes turns to perform their invented ostinato with track 31. (*They might invite the rest of the class to join in singing along with them.*)

  As a class discuss how effective each ostinato part is, and select the four favourites.

- Invite two of the groups to alter the rhythm of their ostinato to match the rhythm of the words for verses 3 and 4, respectively.

- Perform the complete song to track 30 with the chosen ostinato part for each verse (*Everyone sings part 1 when they are not involved in performing their group ostinato part.*)

2 **Invent an alternative ostinato to perform with *I wanna sing scat***

- Sing the first verse ostinato part of *I wanna sing scat*, and ask the children how many different notes are used. (*Three - G D and F.*)

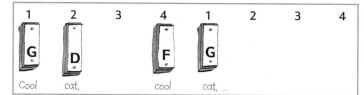

Ask the children what they notice about the last time 'cool cat' is sung. (*It comes slightly later; there is one extra silent beat before it.*)

- Invite individuals to play the ostinato of verse 1 on tuned percussion, keyboard or other melody instrument while the class sing the first voice part with track 31 (*first verse only*).

- Explain that the melody for both parts of the song *I wanna sing scat* is created from these six notes:

Divide the class into groups of four or five and make available as many instruments with these notes as possible. Each group selects three notes, eg , [D G B♭] or [D B♭ C♯]

Each group uses their three notes to invent a new ostinato to sing and play with verse 1.

MOODY MUSIC

1 Discuss the lyrics of two folk songs conveying the same mood p.28 32-33))

- Make copies of the *Song lyrics* photocopiable. Read *The Blue Bell of Scotland* aloud, and ask what the words are about.
  (Someone parted from a person they love. Their love has gone to fight in the war.)

- Do the same with *Danny Boy*.

- Ask which words the children think best convey the mood of parting from someone. Then ask which words the children prefer and why.

- Listen to *The Blue Bell of Scotland* and *Danny Boy* performed as songs *(tracks 32 and 33)*. Ask the children which song they prefer, and whether hearing the music has changed the way they respond to the words. Has the music altered their preference?

- Join in singing with either or both of the songs with the CD.

Background information

- The loving female mourning her lost love who has gone to war forms a backdrop to many folk songs. In *The Blue Bell of Scotland*, King George is probably either King George I (1714-27) or the II (1727-60).

- The melody used for *Danny Boy* was discovered 150 years ago by Jane Ross who was living in Londonderry, and the melody was named *The Londonderry Air*. The words that we use were written in 1913 by Fred Weatherly.

- Blues is a style that originated in America in the early part of the 20th century. Blues often communicates feeling down or low about life but is not necessarily played slowly. A blues piece is also recognised by the chords it uses. The chords that feature in the style formed the basis of later rock and pop music and still feature in song writing today.

2 Discuss the mood, cultural, historical and social meaning of the lyrics of *Hard times blues* 34-35))

- Listen to *Hard times blues* (track 34). Explain that the black singer is describing his feelings of sadness during the Great Depression in America. Work was hard to find particularly for black people.

- Ask when this piece might have been recorded, and why they think that.
  (It was recorded between 1940–1941. The recording is crackly – a lower quality of recording than we are used to today.)

- Ask if the children know what style of music the song belongs to.
  (It is a blues song.)

  From listening to this song, what do they think the characteristics of a blues song are?
  (The mood of a blues song is emotionally down-spirited. Often the theme is about moving on, leaving someone or being left.)

- Invite the children to sing or hum along with the first verse *(track 35)*:

  Hard times, hard times, how long are you gonna stay?
  Hard times, hard times, how long are you gonna stay?
  I'm here today, tomorrow, I may be going away.

3 Make a list of familiar songs that have a historical or social context

- As a class discuss the historical or social context of any familiar songs you know (eg *London bridge is falling down* is about the great fire of London in 1666; *Ring a ring a roses* is about the plague - 'a pocketful of posies' were the herbs people carried with them, 'atishoo atishoo' - the first symptoms of the plague, 'we all fall down' - death.)

- Divide the class into groups. Ask each group to make a list of songs they know and what they are about.
  (Encourage the children to access the worldwide web to find out information about songs they know.)

- Each group shares their ideas with the class.

Song lyrics

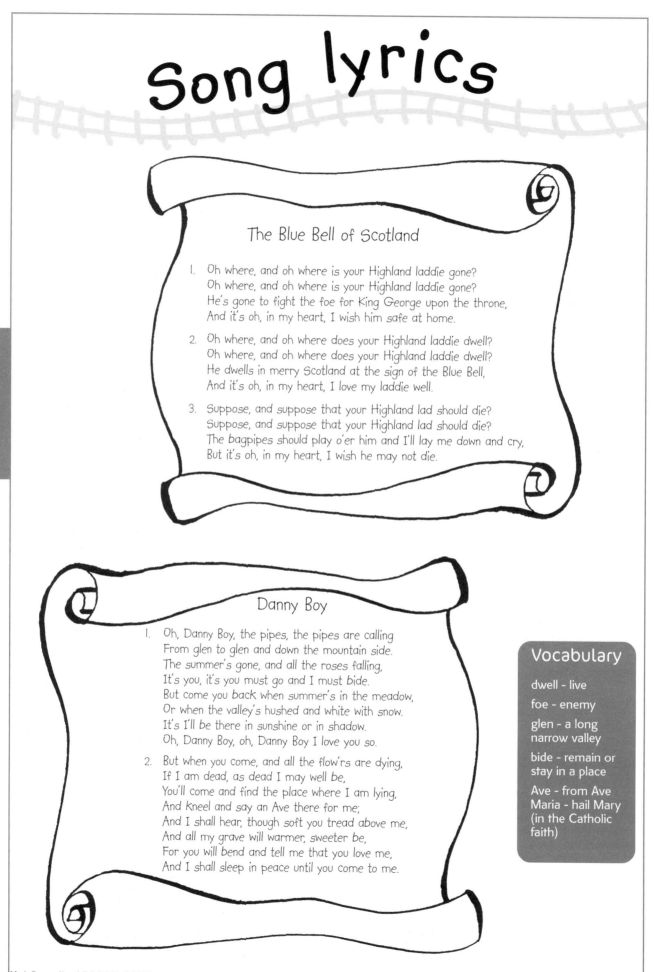

The Blue Bell of Scotland

1. Oh where, and oh where is your Highland laddie gone?
   Oh where, and oh where is your Highland laddie gone?
   He's gone to fight the foe for King George upon the throne,
   And it's oh, in my heart, I wish him safe at home.

2. Oh where, and oh where does your Highland laddie dwell?
   Oh where, and oh where does your Highland laddie dwell?
   He dwells in merry Scotland at the sign of the Blue Bell,
   And it's oh, in my heart, I love my laddie well.

3. Suppose, and suppose that your Highland lad should die?
   Suppose, and suppose that your Highland lad should die?
   The bagpipes should play o'er him and I'll lay me down and cry,
   But it's oh, in my heart, I wish he may not die.

Danny Boy

1. Oh, Danny Boy, the pipes, the pipes are calling
   From glen to glen and down the mountain side.
   The summer's gone, and all the roses falling,
   It's you, it's you must go and I must bide.
   But come you back when summer's in the meadow,
   Or when the valley's hushed and white with snow.
   It's I'll be there in sunshine or in shadow.
   Oh, Danny Boy, oh, Danny Boy I love you so.

2. But when you come, and all the flow'rs are dying,
   If I am dead, as dead I may well be,
   You'll come and find the place where I am lying,
   And kneel and say an Ave there for me;
   And I shall hear, though soft you tread above me,
   And all my grave will warmer, sweeter be,
   For you will bend and tell me that you love me,
   And I shall sleep in peace until you come to me.

Vocabulary

dwell - live

foe - enemy

glen - a long narrow valley

bide - remain or stay in a place

Ave - from Ave Maria - hail Mary (in the Catholic faith)

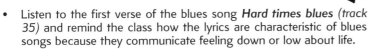

THE BLUES

1 Discuss simple musical features of the blues

- Listen to the first verse of the blues song *Hard times blues (track 35)* and remind the class how the lyrics are characteristic of blues songs because they communicate feeling down or low about life.

- Listen again and all join in singing. Ask the children what they notice about the sung phrases of the song.
  (There are three sung phrases. The first two are the same. The third phrase is different.)

- Ask the class to describe the structure of the first verse.
  (Each sung phrase is followed by a break in which the accompanying instruments are featured.)

- Listen again and count how many beats there are for each sung phrase and each instrumental break.
  (Start counting after the count in for the introduction. Each sung phrase lasts eight beats and each instrumental break another eight beats.)

> **Teaching tips**
> - Chord - three or more notes played at the same time.

2 Learn a blues chord sequence

- Explain that the song *Hard times blues* is accompanied by a chord sequence called a 'twelve bar blues'. A simple blues chord sequence uses three different chords. The chord sequence for *Hard times blues* uses the chords C, F and G:

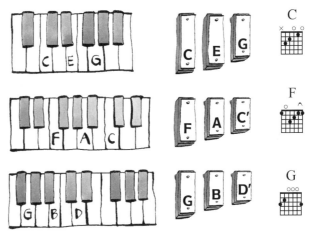

- All follow the twelve bar blues chord sequence shown on the *We've got the blues* photocopiable as you listen to track 36. *(It begins after the introduction and count in.)*

- Notice that there are three lines of chords, one for each line of the song, and that after each sung phrase there is an instrumental break.

3 Practise playing a blues chord sequence

- Divide the tuned resources available between the class to create as many of the three chords as possible – use keyboards, piano, tuned percussion, or guitar (*if you have guitarists*).

- In groups, practice playing the blues chord progression using the *We've got the blues* photocopiable and track 36 for support. Add a steady beat throughout on untuned percussion (*or drum kit if you have anyone in your class who plays*).

- All sing the first verse of *Hard times blues* as you play track 36 again, noticing the changing chords.

> **Teaching tips**
> - Encourage the children to listen to the music and feel where the chord will change. A more natural and more musical effect may be gained by playing by ear in this way than by following the written chord progression on the photocopiable.

We've got the blues

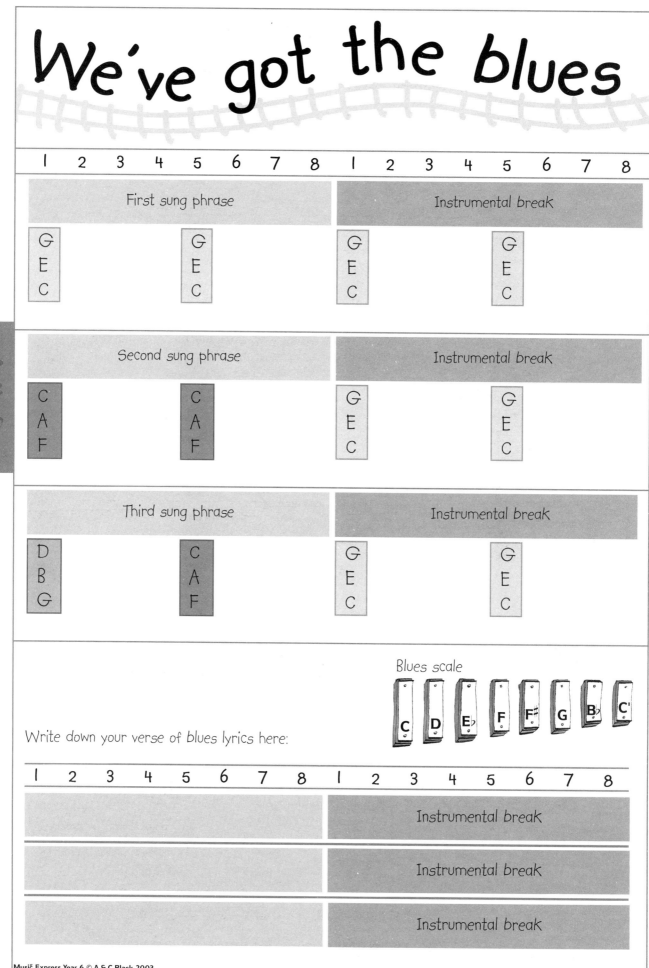

| 1 | 2 | 3 | 4 | 5 | 6 | 7 | 8 | 1 | 2 | 3 | 4 | 5 | 6 | 7 | 8 |

First sung phrase

G E C ... G E C

Instrumental break

G E C ... G E C

Second sung phrase

C A F ... C A F

Instrumental break

G E C ... G E C

Third sung phrase

D B G ... C A F

Instrumental break

G E C ... G E C

Blues scale

C D E♭ F F# G B♭ C'

Write down your verse of blues lyrics here:

| 1 | 2 | 3 | 4 | 5 | 6 | 7 | 8 | 1 | 2 | 3 | 4 | 5 | 6 | 7 | 8 |

Instrumental break

Instrumental break

Instrumental break

Music Express Year 6 © A & C Black 2003
www.acblack.com/musicexpress

BLUES IMPROVISATIONS

1 **Discuss the structure of *Goodbye now* and improvise some blues rhythms in the instrumental breaks** p30 36-38))

- Listen to the extract of *Goodbye now* (*track 37*) and discuss the structure of the verse. (*As with the first verse of **Hard times blues** in lesson 3, each verse consists of two very similar phrases and a third phrase which is different. Each phrase lasts eight beats and is followed by an instrumental break that lasts eight beats.*)

- Explain that the instrumental breaks in a blues song give the players the opportunity to improvise and become more prominent than the singer. Show the children where the instrumental breaks come on the **We've got the blues** photocopiable.

- Notice the instruments played in this recording, and explain that they are characteristic of blues music from the time the song was written. (*Steel stringed guitar, blues harp and washboard played with metal thimbles.*)

- Listen to the rhythmic improvisations on track 38 (*first complete chord sequence*), then invite individuals to improvise in the instrumental breaks of track 36, while the class sing the *Hard times blues* melody. Make use of unusual sound sources, eg tin cans, boxes, metal washers.

Washboard and thimbles

Blues harp

2 **Learn a blues scale and continue exploring blues improvisations** 36/38))

- Explain that there is a particular scale used in blues music called the 'blues scale':

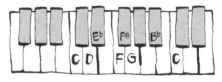

- Using any tuned instruments available (*and instruments that children bring in from home*), set up these groups of notes from the scale:

- Listen to the three examples of melodic improvisation (*following the rhythmic improvisation*) on track 38 (*each using one of the four sets of notes*).

- In pairs or groups, the children take turns to improvise on four notes while the others mark the time by counting them in, then counting to eight (*the length of an instrumental break*).

- Invite individuals to improvise on melody instruments in the instrumental breaks on track 36.

3 **Perform a twelve bar blues** 36))

- You will need to organise the class so that:
  - a group plays the chord sequence;
  - individuals take turns to perform rhythmic or melodic improvisations in the instrumental breaks;
  - a group sings or hums the melody of *Hard times blues*;
  - everyone else fingerclicks or taps a steady beat quietly on impromptu instruments such as chair backs, rulers ...

  Decide on an order for players to perform the improvisations, then perform with or without track 36 for support. (*Repeat the activity several times to give everyone the opportunity to improvise and to practise the chord sequence, sing, or play the steady beat.*)

Teaching tips

- Those who find it tricky to improvise melodically may improvise rhythms on percussion.

- Encourage the children to start by using the given groups of notes, and then to begin to use more notes as their confidence grows.

Songwriter
Exploring lyrics and melody

LYRICAL BLUES

1 Discuss starting points and procedures for creating lyrics for a blues song 36/39

- Explain that groups are going to create their own lyrics and melody for a blues song to sing over the blues chord sequence they learnt to play in the previous lesson.

- Explain that the class will work in groups and create a verse of lyrics first. They will use the structure they learnt in *Hard times blues*:

1	2	3	4	5	6	7	8	1	2	3	4	5	6	7	8
First sung phrase								Instrumental break							
Second sung phrase (repeat of first phrase)								Instrumental break							
Third sung phrase								Instrumental break							

- Remind the class that blues songs are typically about something they might be feeling down about. Discuss subjects for the lyrics from themes such as:
  - everyday school life;
  - topics from local, national or sports news;
  - friends and family.

  All listen to the example of lyrics on track 39, explaining that these were improvised by the singer on the themes suggested above, and noticing again how the first two lines of lyrics are the same, and the third is different.

- Brainstorm some typical opening words *(eg I don't have ... There'll never be ... If I could only ...)* and suggestions for continuing them into a complete line of lyrics: the first and second phrases of the new blues song.

- Invite volunteers to say the phrase rhythmically over the blues chord sequence *(played by an individual on tuned percussion or keyboard, or on track 36)* and get a feel for the placing of the stresses.

  (Play around with the placing of the stresses – there may be several syllables to fit into a beat and several ways to say the phrase. If the lyrics are not falling into place naturally, change them slightly to make a more comfortable fit.)

- As a class, complete the verse by adding a third line of lyrics which is different from the first two *(listen to track 39 again and notice how the third line rounds off the statement made in the first two lines)*. Check that the third line can be said rhythmically and comfortably in the eight beats.

- All say the complete verse rhythmically over the blues chord sequence.

2 Invent lyrics for a blues song in groups p30

- Divide the class into groups to start working on their lyrics. Revise the procedure you used as a class for inventing an opening line of lyrics: deciding on a subject, choosing the opening words and thinking of the continuation, saying them rhythmically over the blues backing.

- The groups continue by:
  - repeating the first sung phrase;
  - inventing a third sung phrase to complete the verse.

  Remind the groups that the third phrase needs to be different from the first two.

- Encourage groups to demonstrate their work in progress, until each has a set of lyrics which they can say rhythmically over the blues chord sequence.

- When each group is happy with their lyrics, they write them on the *We've got the blues* photocopiable.

Teaching tips

- Newspapers are a good place to find starting phrases.
- The children should all have a feel for how long the sung phrases should be by now, but if they are having difficulty with this, play them track 36 and invent an action pattern which alternates every eight beats, eg click fingers for eight beats (sung phrase) then move rhythmically for eight beats (instrumental break), click fingers again, and so on.
- If groups have difficulty writing their own lyrics, encourage them to adapt the class ideas from activity 1.
- Some groups will be confident enough to work with the full blues scale.

3 Create a melody for the group's blues lyrics

- Remind the groups from activity 2 of the melodic improvisations worked on in Lesson 4 activity 2. Explain that they will work in the same way to create a melody for their lyrics.

- Make instruments available as before ensuring that each has four notes from the blues scale:

- Using the rhythm of the lyrics they have invented each group starts to work on creating a melody for their words. Check that the melody captures the mood and style of the blues, asking the class to give constructive evaluation of each group's progress.

THE CLASS BLUES

1 **Work together on a class performance of the groups' blues songs**

- Remind the class of their performance of a twelve bar blues in Lesson 4 and explain that they are going to perform a new twelve bar blues which uses the new verses the groups created in lesson 5. Select children from each of the lesson 5 groups to perform:

    - the blues chord sequence to accompany the song;

    - improvisations on tuned and untuned percussion in the instrumental breaks (*you will need to allocate each break to different instrumentalists*);

    Everyone else fingerclicks or taps a steady beat throughout on soundmakers such as tin cans.

    Rehearse a class performance of the above, ensuring that the sequence can be repeated smoothly and without a break.

- Ask the chord group to prepare the chord sequence below as an introduction:

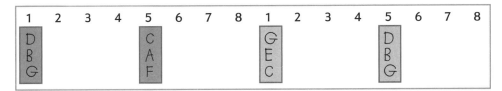

1	2	3	4	5	6	7	8	1	2	3	4	5	6	7	8
D B G				C A F				G E C				D B G			

- When the accompaniment is secure, invite each song group to rehearse their verse in turn with the accompaniment. (*If necessary use the alternating action pattern suggested in Lesson 5 to help the children feel the structure of sung phrase alternating with instrumental break*).

Teaching tips

- An alternative introduction could be as simple as a count in of eight beats with an untuned percussion improvisation.

- Use track 36 to accompany the song if preferred.

- Encourage those children performing the improvisations to play confidently so they can be heard clearly.

- Remind the players that improvisation is intended to be made up on the spot not perfected through rehearsal. Encourage them to be creative in the performance itself.

2 **Rehearse the class blues song and make improvements as necessary**

- Continue working on combining the accompaniment with the singing. Work on moving smoothly from one verse to the next, remembering to count eight beats for the final instrumental break.

- Practise the introduction and entry of the first verse to make sure that:

    - the singers understand when to start singing after the introduction;

    - the singers and accompaniment players are performing in time with the beat.

- Rehearse the complete song with the chord sequence, each group singing their verse in turn.

- When this is secure add improvisations during the instrumental breaks.

3 **Record and evaluate a performance of the class blues song**

- Record a class performance of the blues song. Listen back and discuss:

    - whether the song captured the mood of the blues style;

    - whether all parts were performed confidently;

    - whether all parts kept in time together without speeding up or slowing down.

- If appropriate, invite community musicians to share improvisation ideas with the class and join in a performance of the class blues song.

Teaching tips

- If you have a class who are very confident, perform the song several times to give children the opportunity to play a different part.

LISTENING TO CYCLIC PATTERNS

1 Discuss the use of cyclic patterns in *Stamping tubes* and *Winds on the mountain*

- Listen to *Stamping tubes* (track 40) and explain that different lengths of hollow bamboo are used as instruments in this recording. *(Show the children the picture on the CD-ROM.)*

  Play the track again and all listen for the repeated melodies. Explain that these are examples of cyclic patterns.

- Listen to *Winds on the mountain* (track 41), and discuss the different instruments heard in this piece.
  (Sikus, guitars, mandolins, quena, bombo drum and cha'jchas - see background information.)

  Explain that the opening melody in *Winds on the mountain* is a cyclic pattern repeated throughout. Listen to the cyclic pattern played on its own *(track 42)*, following the melody on the **Cyclic winds** photocopiable.

- Divide the class into pairs or threes to learn the cyclic pattern using tuned percussion and keyboards, notes E G A C' D' and E'.

Teaching tips

- A cyclic pattern is a melodic or rhythmic pattern that is repeated over and over again.
- Cyclic patterns are used in music throughout the world.
- Improvisation means inventing music as you go along.
- Tempo - the speed at which music is performed.
- Harmony - any combination of notes played together.

Background information

- *Stamping tubes* is from the Solomon Islands in the Pacific Ocean. It is performed on twelve different lengths of hollow bamboo, each producing a different pitched note when the open ends are hit on a large smooth stone.
- *Winds on the Mountain* is based on a traditional South American melody.
- Sikus, pronounced see-kooss, are panpipes made from several reeds of graduated length bound together and blown across the top.
- A quena is a type of wooden flute.
- A bombo drum is a hollowed out tree trunk covered with goat skin.
- Cha'jchas - pronounced chah-jazz are rattles made out of goat's hooves.

2 Work out the structure of *Winds on the mountain*

- Listen again to *Winds on the mountain*. Explain that the cyclic pattern is played at the start as a solo on the sikus. Ask which instrument takes over playing the cyclic pattern. *(The quena.)*

- Play the track again and ask how the players add interest to the cyclic pattern when it is repeated.
  (They perform it faster and at a higher pitch. They also develop musical ideas in the pattern to extend it.)

  Explain that playing at a different tempo, improvising and developing repeating ideas are important features of cyclic music.

- Divide the class into pairs or threes, and play track 41 several times for the children to work out the structure of *Winds on the mountain*. The children fill in the structure on the **Cyclic winds** photocopiable. *Answer:*

Instruments:	Played straight or varied?
Solo sikus	Cyclic pattern played once straight
Sikus duet	Second sikus imitates the first - once through cyclic pattern straight
Quena duet	Twice through cyclic pattern in harmony
Quena duet	In harmony - higher pitch and varied
Solo sikus	Cyclic pattern played once straight at faster tempo
Sikus duet	Second sikus imitates first at faster tempo, once straight
Quena duet	Once through cyclic pattern in harmony at faster tempo then varied

3 Identify cyclic patterns in *Baris gede 'bandrangan'* and improvise drum rhythms

- Listen to *Baris gede 'bandrangan'*. Explain that this piece contains several cyclic patterns all played at once.

  Play the track again, and invite individuals to identify the cyclic patterns for the class by demonstrating the pitch with their hands as the music is played.
  (The higher-pitched instruments play melodic cyclic patterns which are made of many repeated notes. The lower-sounding instruments perform melodic cyclic patterns made of much longer notes.)

- Listen again and ask the children to follow then describe the drum part.
  (The drummer improvises throughout, and leads the performance by signalling to the other players when to play loudly or quietly.)

- Play the track again and invite individuals to take turns improvising rhythms on hand drums throughout.

Background information

- *Baris gede 'bandrangan'* is a modern piece of gamelan music from Bali, composed by I Wayan Beratha.
- Gamelan is the name of a group of instruments (mainly tuned percussion) as well as the music itself. Most gamelan have about twenty players, but some are much larger.
- A *baris gede* is a ritual spear dance for men; this one is called 'bandrangan' after the tassel attached to the spear's handle.

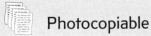
Cyclic winds

Cyclic pattern:

E'
C'   C C' C'   C'
A A   A   A   G
E

E'   D E' D E'   C'   C' D E'   D C'
                                      A

Write down below how many times this cyclic pattern is repeated and how it is varied.
The first two repetitions have been filled in for you.

Instruments:	Played straight or varied?
Solo sikus	Cyclic pattern played once straight
Sikus duet	Second sikus imitates the first - once through cyclic pattern straight

INTRODUCING GAMELAN

1 Listen to examples of gamelan music and learn about the instruments

- Listen again to *Baris gede 'bandrangan'* (*track 43*) and explain that it is a piece of modern Balinese gamelan music. Discuss what is meant by gamelan, and show the children the photographs of some gamelan instruments on the CD-ROM:

  – gongs (*pic 3*);
  (*The three nearest are called 'kempul'; the second largest is the 'gong suwukan'; the largest is the 'gong ageng'.*)

  – kenong and sarons (*pic 4*);
  (*The instrument in the foreground is the 'kenong' and to the right are a row of 'sarons'.*)

  – bonang barung (*pic 5*);
  (*This instrument is the 'bonang'. It is called barung because it is the larger.*)

  – bonang panerus (*pic 6*);
  (*This instrument is another 'bonang'.*)

  Explain that the gamelan is led by a drummer, and sometimes also includes a flute and singing.

- Listen to a piece of traditional Javanese gamelan music, *Bendrong* (*track 44*). Revise what is meant by the term cyclic pattern (*see lesson 1*), then listen to *Bendrong* again, focusing in particular on the higher-pitched melodic cyclic pattern which the children are going to learn.

Background information

- The gamelan originated in Java and Bali and has featured in their traditional way of life for hundreds of years.

- Each gamelan is hand made and each has its own tuning which is either a five-note scale 'slendro' or a seven-note scale 'pelog'. The tuning is not the same as western European tuning. This unit will use the notes F G A B and C' to represent approximately the five-note scale used in *Bendrong*.

- The music in *Bendrong* is intended to lift a spell under which Yuyu Kangkang, the river crab, is held working in a swamp.

2 Learn a melodic cyclic pattern by ear using voices and tuned percussion

- Explain that the class is going to learn a simplified version of the *Bendrong* cyclic pattern which they listened to in activity 1. Explain that classroom tuned percussion instruments will sound similar in pitch but not exactly the same as those in *Bendrong*.

  Explain that gamelan melodies are traditionally learnt by ear, but can be represented by numbers to help those new to gamelan music. The notes of the scale the children will be using are:

F	G	A	B	C'
1	2	3	5	6

- Practise singing the first half of the *Bendrong* cyclic pattern using track 45 and the *Cyclic melody* photocopiable until everyone is confident.

  6 1 2 1 6 1 2 1 6 1 2 1 6 2 1 2

- When everyone is confident singing this, encourage as many children as possible to practise playing it on tuned percussion instruments (*notes F G C'*) with track 45.
  (*The rest of the class add support by singing.*)

3 Rehearse and perform the first half of the *Bendrong* cyclic melody

- When the class is confident rehearsing with track 45, rehearse without the CD.

  Invite a volunteer to be the conductor. Groups of children take turns performing the cyclic pattern on tuned percussion (*everyone else sings*).

  Collect together as many sets of tuned percussion notes F G and C' as you can for this activity.

  The conductor chooses an appropriate tempo, and taps the beat on a drum to indicate the chosen speed.
  (*Decide in advance a suitable signal for the conductor to start and stop the players. The conductor also marks the beat to maintain a steady speed.*)

Teaching tips

- Explore sounds on a keyboard to find a metallophone, gong or gamelan sound.

- If your tuned percussion selection is limited, encourage children to take turns playing the instruments.

- There is no number four because it is not involved in this five-note scale.

- Some children may find it helpful to label the relevant notes 1 2 and 6.

Cyclic melody

First half

C' F G F C' F G F
6   1 2 1 6   1 2 1

C' F G F C' G F G
6   1 2 1 6   2 1 2

Second half

A F G F A F G F
3 1 2 1 3 1 2 1

A F G F A G F G
3 1 2 1 3 2 1 2

Music Express Year 6 © A & C Black 2003
www.acblack.com/musicexpress

GAMELAN MELODY

1 **Learn the complete gamelan melodic cyclic pattern** p37  46))

- All revise the first half of the *Bendrong* melodic cyclic pattern learnt in Lesson 2, then add the second half, using track 46 and the *Cyclic melody* photocopiable.
  (Notice that the second half follows the same pattern as the first half but starting on the note A instead of C'.)

- When all can sing the complete cyclic pattern confidently, rehearse playing it on tuned percussion *(notes F G A C')* with track 46.
  (As in Lesson 2 activity 3, the children should take turns practising the cyclic pattern on the tuned percussion you have available. The class supports by singing.)

  A conductor marks the steady beat throughout on a drum.

> ## Background information
>
> - When playing the gamelan, the players use a damping technique to stop (*close*) the sound. The player stops the sound by holding the bar of the note just played while playing the next note. One hand is always following the melody, damping the sound behind it.

> ## Teaching tips
>
> - Prepare as many sets of tuned percussion with notes F G A and C' as you can before the lesson, dividing them into collections of higher-pitched and lower-pitched instruments.
>
> - In gamelan music the smaller, higher-pitched instruments tend to play faster-moving parts than the lower-sounding instruments. Use the higher-pitched instruments to play the decoration.
>
> - If your resources are limited, encourage groups to share instruments. Include keyboard sounds as well as tuned percussion.
>
> - Some children might find it helpful to label the notes 1 2 3 and 6 as before.

2 **Practise adding decoration to the gamelan cyclic melody** p39 47)) 4

- Explain that gamelan players often decorate a melody on a different instrument by playing each note just before it is played by the main instrument. This is shown on the *Cyclic extras* photocopiable, and demonstrated on track 47 and videoclip 4.
  (On track 47 and the videoclip, one person plays the cyclic melody all the way through twice, the first time alone then joined by the second player, decorating the melody. The second player starts the decoration ahead of the main melody.)

- As a whole class, or in groups of three or four, practise decorating the melody. You will need someone to do each of the following:

  – tap the beat throughout *(this might be on two different instruments as in videoclip 4);*

  – play the cyclic melody on a lower-pitched instrument;

  – play the decoration on a higher-pitched instrument.

  (Encourage the children to play by ear rather than by reading the photocopiable.)

  Encourage each group to swap parts regularly to give everyone the opportunity to practise all of them.

3 **Learn an accompanying cyclic pattern to perform with the decorated cyclic melody** p39 48))

- Learn an accompanying cyclic pattern to perform with the decorated cyclic melody using the *Cyclic extras* photocopiable and track 48.
  (The accompanying cyclic pattern requires two notes to be played at the same time.)

  Invite individuals to take turns performing the accompanying part on tuned percussion with track 48.

- Divide the class into groups of four to rehearse the accompanying cyclic pattern with the melody and its decoration, and beat rehearsed in activity 2. You will need someone to do each of the following:

  – tap the beat throughout *(as in activity 2);*

  – perform the cyclic melody on a lower-pitched instrument;

  – play the decoration on a higher-pitched instrument;

  – play the accompanying cyclic pattern on a low-pitched instrument.

- Invite groups to perform to the class.

Bonang barung

Cyclic extras

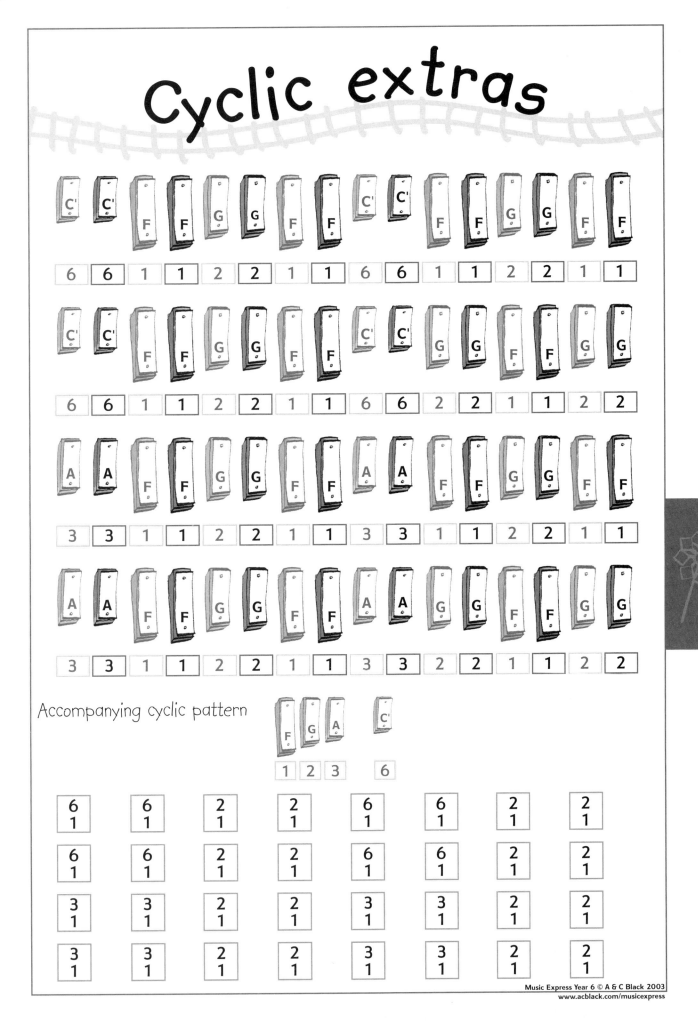

Accompanying cyclic pattern

Music Express Year 6 © A & C Black 2003
www.acblack.com/musicexpress

Cyclic patterns
Exploring rhythm and pulse

ADDING CONTRAST

1 **Learn two cyclic patterns in** *Baris gede 'bandrangan'*

- Listen again to *Baris gede 'bandrangan' (track 43)* and remind the class that this is a modern gamelan cyclic piece.

- Learn to play two of the cyclic patterns which are repeated throughout the track with the *Cyclic patterns* photocopiable and track 49. You will need:

  – medium-pitched instruments: notes D E♭ and F to play cyclic pattern 1;

  – low-pitched instruments: notes C and D to play cyclic pattern 2.

- When everyone is confident performing with track 49, rehearse without the CD support. Invite a group to mark the steady beat on hand drums as indicated on the photocopiable.

> **Teaching tips**
> - You will need as many tuned resources as possible to give children a chance to play together.
> - Divide your tuned percussion and keyboard resources into two sizes: medium-pitched and low-pitched.

2 **Compare the performances of *Baris gede 'bandrangan'* and *Bendrong* and discuss the use of contrast and variety**

- When the class is familiar with the two main cyclic patterns in *Baris gede 'bandrangan'* through performing them with track 49, all listen again to track 43 to identify the cyclic patterns within the piece.

  Ask whether the two cyclic patterns are performed throughout the track.
  (No - they do not play in the introduction, but having started they continue throughout.)

  Discuss what else happens in the piece.
  (Higher-pitched tuned instruments perform faster cyclic patterns, a drum adds improvisations, and other untuned percussion instruments such as rattles and shakers join in at times. There are also changes in dynamics which are directed by the drummer, and variations in the number of instruments playing at any particular time.)

- Listen again to *Bendrong* (track 44) and discuss how this piece compares with the more modern piece, *Baris gede 'bandrangan'*.
  (There is less contrast and variety within Bendrong. The same instruments play throughout and the overall dynamics remain at the same level. A drum and a high-pitched bell improvise rhythm patterns throughout.)

- Explain that in the next activities the children are going to add contrast and variety to the *Bendrong* cyclic pattern using ideas for this from *Baris gede 'bandrangan'*. Ask the class for their suggestions *(eg add extra cyclic patterns, add drum improvisation and rhythm patterns; add extra instruments; include changes in dynamics, numbers of instruments playing, tempo ...).*

3 **Develop ideas for adding contrast and variety to the** *Bendrong* **cyclic pattern**

- Divide the class into groups and explain that the children are going to develop ideas from activity 2 for including in a performance of the *Bendrong* cyclic pattern.
  (You might want to allocate a specific task to each group, eg composing a new cyclic pattern or working out how to control changes of dynamics perhaps using a drum signal. Alternatively the children may be more creative if left to their own devices.)

- Each group will need access to the tuned notes F G A B and C', and other untuned percussion instruments.

- The groups make a note of their ideas for next lesson. Some may find it helpful to record their ideas on audio cassette.

> **Teaching tips**
> - Remind the children that the lower-pitched instruments tend to perform cyclic patterns which are slower moving, while higher-pitched instruments perform cyclic patterns or rhythms which are faster moving.
> - Give groups access to the CD tracks for inspiration, especially *Baris gede 'bandrangan'* and *Bendrong*.

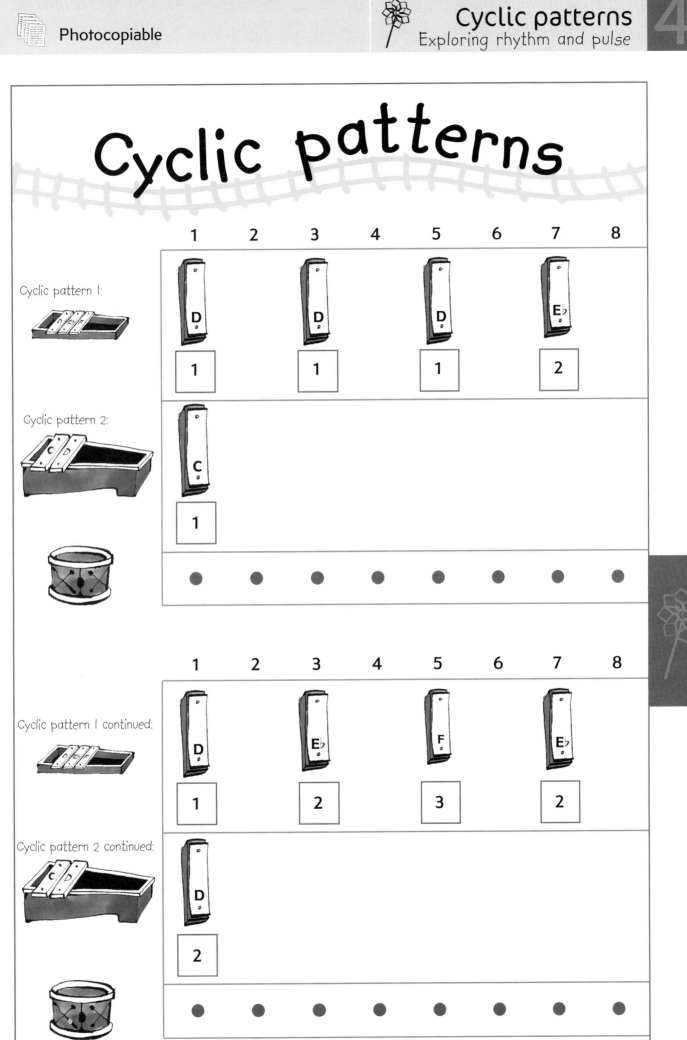

Cyclic patterns

Cyclic pattern 1:

Cyclic pattern 2:

Cyclic pattern 1 continued:

Cyclic pattern 2 continued:

Cyclic patterns
Exploring rhythm and pulse

GAMELAN STYLE

1 **Continue developing ideas for adding contrast and variety to the *Bendrong* cyclic pattern**

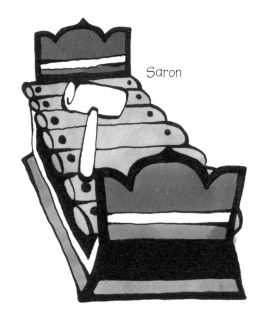

Saron

- Remind the class that they are working in groups to explore ideas to to go with the *Bendrong* cyclic pattern. They are aiming to add extra interest and decoration in the style of the modern gamelan piece, *Baris gede 'bandrangan'*.

- Each group revises their ideas from last lesson and continues their exploration. Encourage each group to consider:

  - inventing a new cyclic pattern using any of the notes F G A B and C';

  - including a more elaborate improvised drum part;

  - adding other untuned percussion instruments to the performance;

  - finding a way to alter dynamics, eg with drum signals;

  - finding a way to vary the tempo;

  - developing the cyclic melody through improvisation for part of the piece.

2 **Discuss ideas found for developing the cyclic pattern and plan a performance**

- Each group presents their ideas to the class.

- As a class, discuss which ideas would work well together to create a piece of music.

- Decide whether you will work as a class or in large groups *(this will depend on your available resources and how confident your class is working in groups)* and begin to plan your performance. You will need to consider:

  - whether the cyclic melody learnt in weeks 2 and 3 will continue throughout;

  - whether you will include the accompanying cyclic pattern learnt in lesson 3;

  - how many other cyclic patterns to include;

  - whether any of the other cyclic patterns will continue throughout;

  - whether to decorate any of the cyclic patterns for some of the performance;

  - how to begin and finish the piece;

  - whether to include drum improvisations or signals;

  - whether to include any other untuned percussion instruments;

  - how to keep all the performers in time together.

3 **Rehearse for a performance of the adapted *Bendrong* cyclic pattern**

- Once you have decided what to include in the performance of the *Bendrong* cyclic pattern, rehearse the piece.
  (If you are working as a whole class, it might be helpful to write a plan on the board which everyone can see.)

  Encourage the children to listen carefully as they rehearse and offer suggestions for improvement. They might like to add fresh ideas, inspired by the rehearsing, as well as abandon ideas that are not so effective.

- Record a work-in-progress performance to listen to next lesson.

Teaching tips

- You might decide to appoint a conductor to direct the performance, or invite a confident child to signal changes on a drum as well as maintain a steady beat.

- When rehearsing the piece do not always start from the beginning each time. Instead rehearse particular sections of the piece, eg the ending.

PERFORMING GAMELAN

1 **Appraise the work in progress and use the observations to make improvements**

* Listen to the class or group recordings of work in progress made at the end of last lesson and appraise them as a class. Consider whether:
  - everyone is performing in time with each other;
  - there is a balance between the volume of the parts, except when some are intentionally louder;
  - everyone is satisfied with the ideas they have included;
  - the class is happy with the amount of contrast and variation in the piece.
* Continue rehearsing the piece and making improvements.

Kenong

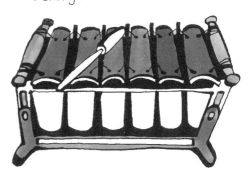

Teaching tips

* Make sure the instruments playing the same part are positioned together.
* Set out your performance area so that everyone can see each other, in particular the lead drummer or conductor *(if you are using one)*.
* Listen to the performance of *Bendrong* on the CD and compare it with your own performance.

2 **Record and appraise the class or group adaptations of the *Bendrong* cyclic pattern**

* When the class or groups can confidently perform their pieces and are happy with their work, record a performance.
  (Remember to start and finish with silence.)
* Listen to the recording and celebrate the progress the children have made. Encourage individuals to suggest aspects of each performance they considered the most effective.

3 **Perform the piece for a special occasion**

* When you have an opportunity, rehearse and perform the class or group pieces for a special occasion such as a school concert, school assembly or open evening.

Gongs

SILVER AND GOLD

1 Listen to and discuss the two-part song *Silver and gold*

- Listen to *Silver and gold*, then ask the children to describe the mood of the song.
  (eg cheerful, upbeat, positive ...)

- Ask what gives the song its mood.
  (The words, the tempo, the accompaniment, the melody and rhythm, and how they all combine.)

- Listen again, pausing the CD at the end of a section to ask these questions:

  – what methods and places for finding treasure are suggested at the beginning?
    (Using a metal detector, digging with a spade into the ground, finding a pirate's ship on the ocean.)

  – why don't you need to seek treasure with these methods and in these places?
    (Because, if you open your eyes, you see that your world is full of friends who are your treasures.)

  – what well-known saying is sung in the chorus? What does it mean?
    ('Make new friends but keep the old, the one is silver and the other gold.' It encourages you to make new friends, but says that old friends are just as important.)

  – what friendship problems are described in the second verse, and how does the song suggest dealing with them?
    (Friends argue and fight about trivial things; friends let you down and leave you upset. To save the friendship, the song suggests forgiving and forgetting.)

  – how are the words performed in the section after the second chorus?
    (The words are chanted.)

2 Learn to sing the backing vocal to the chorus of *Silver and gold* with actions

- Use the *I love my friends* photocopiable and CD track 2 to teach the backing vocals and actions for the chorus.

- Encourage the children to:

  – be ready to sing after the third beat (*see photocopiable*);

  – articulate clearly the 'fr' of 'friends';

  – sustain 'friends' and 'gold' for their full four beats;

  – be ready for the third 'friends' on the higher note;

  – enjoy singing 'yeah!';

  – communicate with a positive, happy sound;

  – perform the actions with enthusiasm.

Background information

- *Silver and Gold* is a two-part song about the value of friendship. The songwriter, Ana Sanderson, based it on the well-known saying: 'Make new friends but keep the old, the one is silver and the other gold'.

- It is written in popular style; the second voice part is a backing vocal to the main voice part.

3 Perform the backing vocal with a recording of the chorus

- Sing the backing vocals for the chorus with track 3.
  (Notice that the backing vocals begin before the main chorus melody.)

- Practise this several times. Focus on:

  – singing the backing vocals in time with the same steady beat of the chorus;

  – singing the words with clear articulation;

  – singing happily.

Teaching tip

- When the children are singing the backing vocals at the same time as the chorus, encourage them to be aware of the chorus rather than block it out.

I love my friends

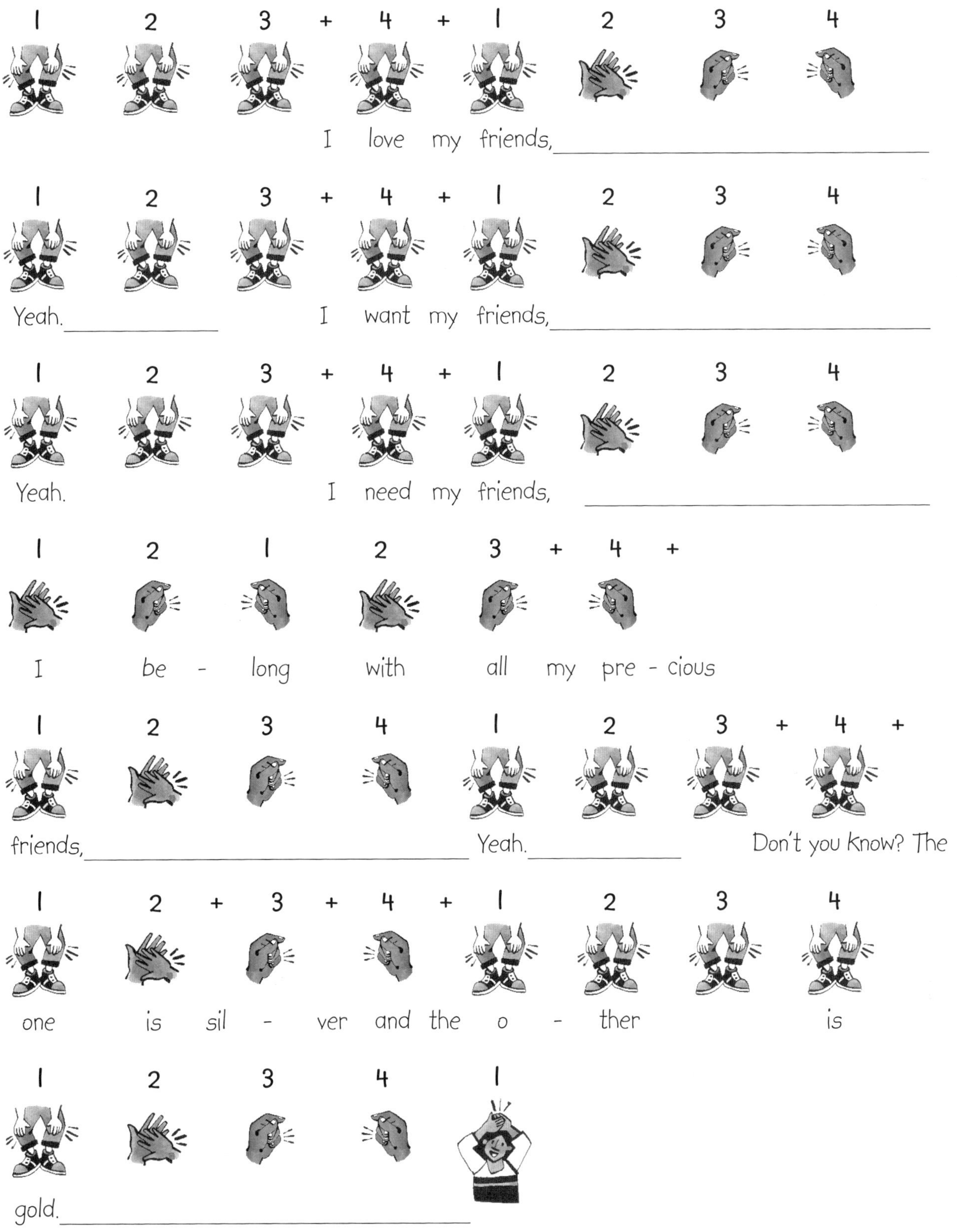

| 1 | 2 | 3 | + | 4 | + | 1 | 2 | 3 | 4 |

I   love   my   friends,_____

| 1 | 2 | 3 | + | 4 | + | 1 | 2 | 3 | 4 |

Yeah._____   I   want   my   friends,_____

| 1 | 2 | 3 | + | 4 | + | 1 | 2 | 3 | 4 |

Yeah.   I   need   my   friends,   _____

| 1 | 2 | 1 | 2 | 3 | + | 4 | + |

I   be - long   with   all   my   pre - cious

| 1 | 2 | 3 | 4 | 1 | 2 | 3 | + | 4 | + |

friends,_____   Yeah._____   Don't you know? The

| 1 | 2 | + | 3 | + | 4 | + | 1 | 2 | 3 | 4 |

one   is   sil - ver   and   the   o - ther   is

| 1 | 2 | 3 | 4 | 1 |

gold._____

Music Express Year 6 © A & C Black 2003
www.acblack.com/musicexpress

45

MAKE NEW FRIENDS

1 Learn the first verse and chorus of *Silver and gold*

- Teach the first verse of *Silver and gold* using CD track 4, then the chorus using track 5.

Vs 1 You don't need a metal detector to find the greatest treasure,
You don't need a spade to dig deep into the ground,
You don't need to find a pirate's ship sailing across the ocean blue,
All you've got to do is open your eyes and look around.
Your world is full of treasures,
Your treasures are your friends; so:

Ch Make new friends but keep the old.
The one is silver and the other is gold.
That's the wisest thing I've been told;
Make new friends but keep the old.
The one is silver and the other is gold.

Teaching tips

When teaching the first verse of the song, pay particular attention to:

- articulating the words clearly, energetically and rhythmically (especially the words 'metal detector', 'greatest treasure', 'spade to dig deep', 'pirate's ship', 'open your eyes')
- sustaining the vowels of words such as 'around', 'friends', 'so'
- knowing when to start after the introduction.

When teaching the chorus, encourage the children to:

- keep their energy levels up when the phrase starts low but finishes high (eg 'Make new friends but keep the old');
- keep their energy up for the high note on the word 'That's';
- sustain the vowel sounds of words such as 'around', 'friends', 'so', 'told' and 'gold'.

2 Learn percussion parts to accompany the chorus

- Revise the backing vocals and actions for the chorus of *Silver and gold* (see Lesson 1 activity 2).

- Divide the class into three groups to practise the percussion accompaniments for the chorus using tracks 6-7 and the *Friendly percussion* and *Tuneful treasure* photocopiables. You will need:

  – group 1: guiros, tambourines, snare drum and bass drum (or other similar instruments);

  – group 2: bass xylophones - notes B♭ E♭ F and G;

  – group 3: glockenspiels - notes F A♭ B♭ D♭.

  Practise the untuned percussion parts using track 6 and the tuned percussion parts using track 7.

- Each group performs its percussion part while the rest of the class sing the backing vocals of the chorus and perform the actions.

Teaching tips

- Allow sufficient practice time.
- Encourage the children to keep time and to play rhythmically.
- Be ready to come in on time with the percussion parts. Notice that the practice count in (tracks 6-7) begins on the final word of the verse: 'So'. Be ready.
- Remind the children of the introduction.
- Encourage those singing to sing with clear articulation.

3 Perform the chorus of *Silver and gold* with the percussion accompaniment, backing vocals and actions

- Rehearse the chorus, using the appropriate part of track 5, with the class divided into these groups:

  – tuned and untuned percussion players;

  – a small group of more confident singers to sing the backing vocals with actions;

  – the rest of the class singing the main chorus.

  Rehearse two groups at a time, before attempting all three groups performing at once.

- When everyone is confident, rehearse the verse and chorus with the backing track *(track 8)*. All sing the verse and then divide into groups to perform the chorus as rehearsed.

- Encourage a group of individuals to listen to the performance and feedback afterwards on whether everyone was playing in time together and whether there was a good balance between all the parts.
  (Could the singing be heard clearly above the accompanying parts?)

Friendly percussion

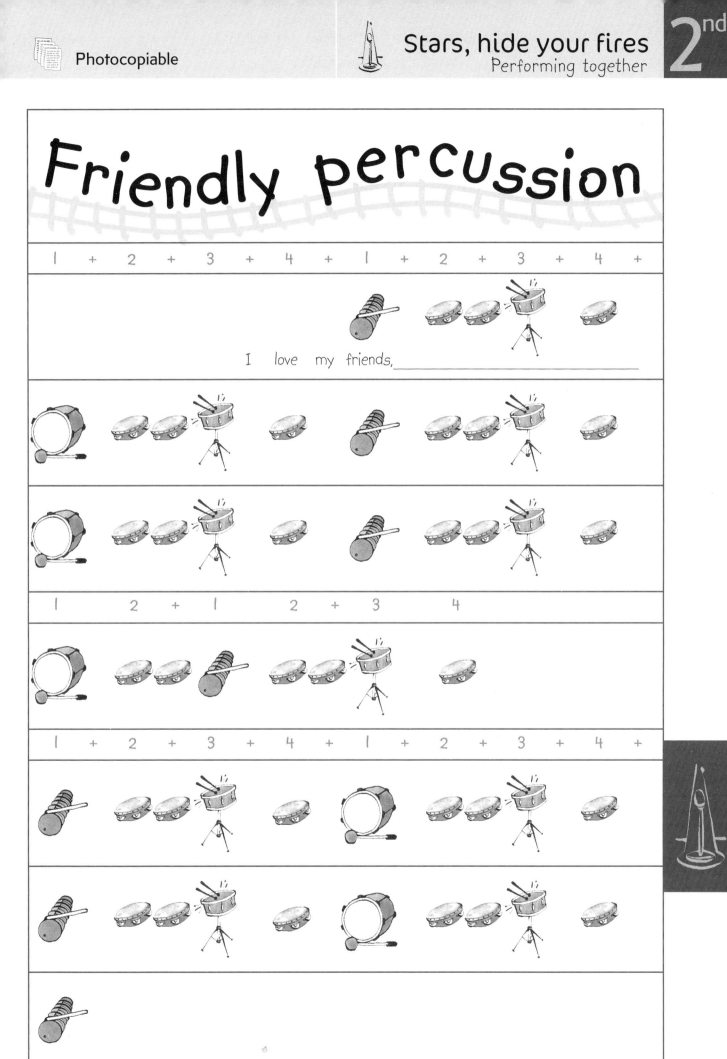

I love my friends,

Stars, hide your fires
Performing together

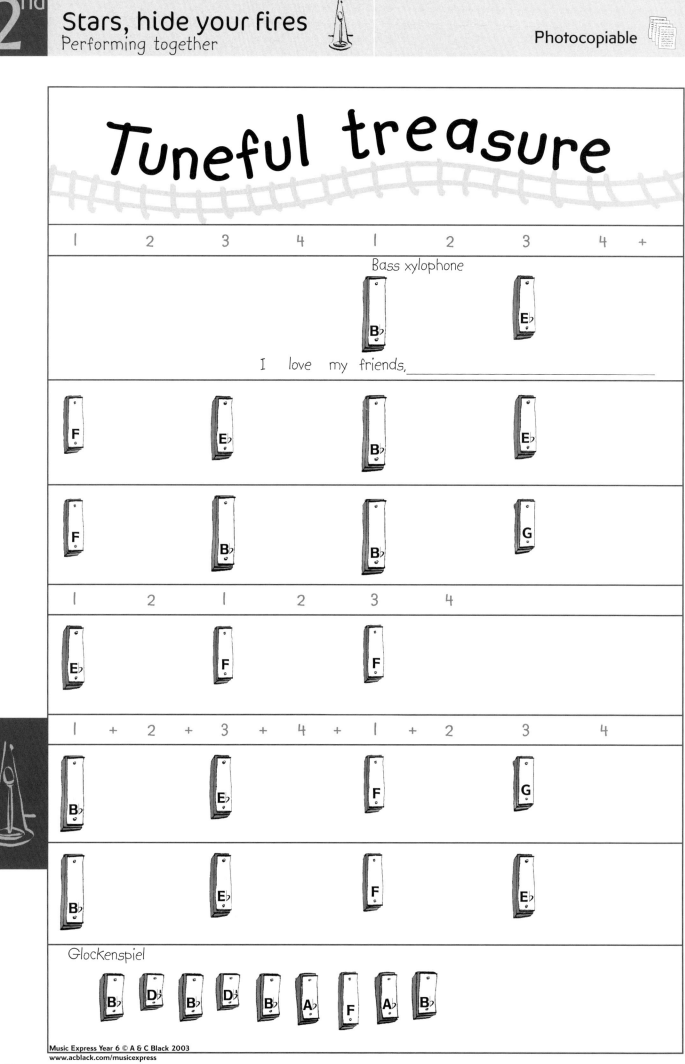

Tuneful treasure

REMEMBER YOUR FRIENDS

1 **Learn to sing the second verse of *Silver and gold***

- Revise singing the first verse and chorus of *Silver and gold*, then teach the second verse using track 9.

Vs2 Sometimes friends will argue and fight about things
      which aren't important,
Sometimes friends can let you down, leaving you upset.
If you feel that you don't understand, yet you don't
      want to lose your friend,
All you've got to do is try to forgive and to forget.
Just try to make amends.
Remember they're your friends. And:

Pay particular attention to:

- beginning and ending phrases together;
- articulating the words clearly (eg 'argue and fight', 'feel that you don't understand', 'try to forgive' ...);
- breathing at the ends of phrases.

Teaching tips

- You will require plenty of space in which the children can work.
- Select the most appropriate activities according to your pupils' abilities and the resources and space available to you. It may be that you have new ideas that can be incorporated into the performance.
- Children who learn violin, cello, flute, clarinet or recorder could take the parts (printed out from the CD-ROM) to their next instrumental lesson to practise.

2 **Learn the two rap parts from *Silver and gold***

- Teach the two parts of the rap separately using track 10.

Rap - first part	*Rap - second part*
Make new friends	Yeah!
but keep the old,	Yeah!
The one is silver	Silver!
And the other gold.	Gold! Yeah!
That's the wisest	Wisest!
Thing I've been told	Told! Yeah!
About my silver and gold!	Yeah! Silver and gold!

- Divide into two groups to practise performing the two parts together. Be careful to:
  - chant the words rhythmically and with enthusiasm;
  - maintain a steady beat *(don't rush)*;
  - work on ensemble and balance.

3 **Work in small groups on additional contributions to the performance** p47 p48 p50 11 ♪

- Give the children the opportunity to try different accompaniment ideas for the song, alongside those learnt last lesson.

Working individually or in groups, give everyone the choice of:

- learning the second voice part for verses 1 and 2 *(track 11)*;
- practising the tuned and untuned accompaniments from the *Friendly percussion* and *Tuneful treasure* photocopiables;
- practising the descant recorder, treble recorder, flute, clarinet, violin and cello parts available on the CD-ROM;
- inventing untuned rhythm patterns following directions on the *Rhythm blocks* photocopiable ;
- inventing lyrics for a new rap section for the song;
- devising movement and dance ideas for part of the performance.

Rhythm blocks

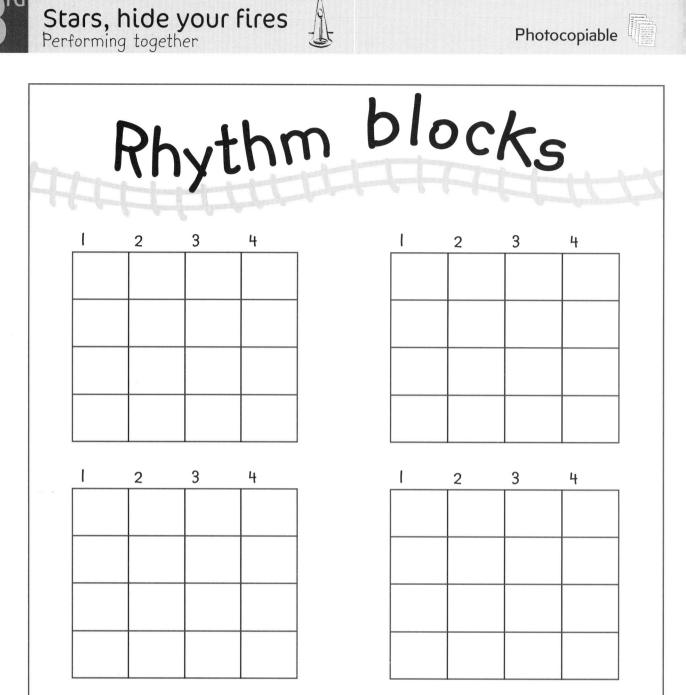

Invent four-beat rhythm patterns

- Choose four untuned percussion instruments.
- Experiment playing them on different beats and combining their sounds in different ways.
- Write down your patterns in the empty rhythm blocks above.
- Repeat the patterns over and over to create ostinati.
- Experiment playing your ostinati to accompany different parts of the song.

eg

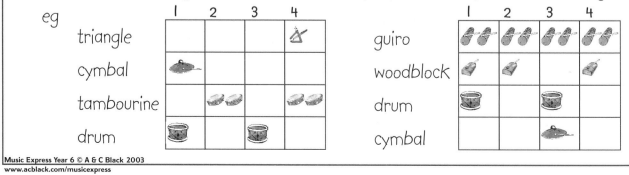

Music Express Year 6 © A & C Black 2003
www.acblack.com/musicexpress

COMPLETE THE SONG

1 Continue the work begun in the previous lesson on other contributions to the performance

- Each group or individual continues rehearsing their additional contributions to the performance.

- Encourage each individual or group to perform to the class, and encourage the class to give positive feedback.

2 Decide when to include additional contributions in the song

- Decide as a class who will perform what in the final performance. Consider:

  – whether you will perform with or without the backing track;

  – how many singers are needed for each part of the song and who they will be;

  – which accompaniment ideas and composed rhythm blocks to include and when, making sure the singing can always be heard;

  – whether to replace the rap with a new rap;

  – whether there are dance ideas which the class considers effective to include in the performance;

  – whether a conductor will be needed for the performance.

Try out your ideas. Practise singing parts of the song with different accompaniments and discuss which are the most effective.

Teaching tips
- Notice that the second voice part begins as an echo of the first.
- Notice that the ending slows down and then picks up speed again.
- When practising the song all the way through, encourage the singers who have been practising the second part in the verses to include them.

3 Learn both voice parts of the coda and practise singing the song all the way through in two parts

- Teach the first part of the coda using track 12.

First part (sing twice)
Silver and gold,
My new friends and old.
They are my greatest treasure,
They are my hours of pleasure.
How sad it would be if
I never could be with
My most precious treasure,
My silver and gold.

Second part (sing twice)
Silver and gold,
My new friends and old.
Ooh
Ooh
How sad it would be if
I never could be with
My most precious,
Silver and gold.

- When everyone is confident singing the first part, teach everyone the second voice part using track 13.

- Practise both parts together using track 13 again.

- When everyone is confident singing the coda, sing the song all the way through using either track 1 (*performance track*) or track 8 (*backing track*). Pay particular attention to:

  – remembering the words in the correct order;

  – concentrating throughout;

  – communicating the words and their meaning to a would-be audience;

  – articulating the words clearly;

  – looking focussed and committed while singing;

  – balance between the two voice parts.

PREPARE TO PERFORM

1 **Discuss non-musical factors that contribute to a good performance and make a performance plan**

- As a class think about when and where you will be performing the song. Discuss:

  - The performance space
    Is it big or small? Is the audience near to or far away from the performers? Is there a stage? ...

  - Dress code
    What should you wear - school uniform, all wearing the same but not school uniform, eg coloured shirts, costumes? ...

- Decide on a plan for the performance and write it down with as much detail as possible to remember for next lesson, eg

Introduction	CD backing track + group I rhythm block accompaniment
Verse I	Details of who is singing the first part and who the second. Flute, violin and cello parts.
Chorus I	Details of who is singing the first part and who the second. I love my friends actions. Friendly percussion accompaniment.
Verse 2	Details of who is singing the first part and who the second. Descant and treble recorder. Bass xylophone and glockenspiel parts.
Chorus 2	Details of who is singing the first part and who the second. I love my friends actions. Tuneful treasure accompaniment.
Rap	New rap - details of performers. Dance composition.
Coda	Details of who is singing the first part and who the second. Group 2 rhythm block accompaniment.

- Decide where everyone will be positioned for the performance. Check that:

  - everyone will be able to see the conductor (if you are using one);

  - instrumentalists will be able to sit or stand comfortably in order to play without strain;

  - instrumentalists playing from copies can see them comfortably.

  (You might like to sketch a map of the performance area.)

Teaching tips

- The performance plan should contain any information that you want written in a form that is useful to you, eg who is performing what and when.
- Choose your own notation: names, words, symbols, pictures, music notation.
- You might need to make alterations to the performance plan as you rehearse.

2 **Put all the parts of the performance together**

- Decide whether children will join in the singing when they are not performing their accompaniment. Make sure everyone is clear about what they are doing and when.

- Rehearse the song all the way through and in short sections several times until everyone is confident. Check that:

  - everyone comes in at the right time;

  - all parts are performed in time with each other;

  - the balance between all the parts is good, and the singers can be heard clearly;

  - everyone is silent before they start and after they finish.

3 **Make improvements to the performance**

- Continue refining the performance so that all children are giving their best.

- Make a recording of a complete run-through of *Silver and gold*. Listen back with the children and discuss ideas for improvement.

PERFORMANCE

1 Hold a dress rehearsal or final run-through

- Set up the performance area - position any chairs, instruments and music stands where needed, and make sure any music parts needed are in an appropriate place.
  (Make sure the performance area looks tidy.)

- Have a walk-through rehearsal. Practise:

  - walking into the performance area;
    (Practise walking on, in order, quietly and efficiently and getting into position sensibly.)

  - acknowledging the applause;
    (Will the conductor bow? Will everyone stand still and smile at the audience after walking onto the stage, and before sitting down to perform? Will everyone bow, if so practise bowing at the same time.)

  - starting the song;
    (Practise waiting for silence from the audience before starting the song.)

  - sitting and holding instruments silently when not playing;
    (Make sure everyone knows when to pick up their instrument ready to play and can do so as quietly as possible. Practise sitting without fidgeting.)

  - holding the stillness at the end of the performance;
    (Practise the last few notes of the song, and staying still and silent until the applause starts.)

  - acknowledging the applause;
    (Practise all standing up together if seated, and bowing if the children decide they would like to.)

  - walking off the performance area.
    (Practise walking off, in order, quietly and efficiently after the applause has finished.)

Teaching tips

- Remind the children that they only get one chance at a performance and so they will need to concentrate.

- Point out that the children are on show the entire time and should be on their best behaviour.

- When you rehearse, notice whether the performance area is particularly echoey. If so, encourage the singers to articulate the words more crisply than usual.

- If any children are bringing instruments in from home to play, ask if their teachers could check they are in tune before the performance.

2 Refine the performance 🔊 8))

- Rehearse a performance of the song. Walk into the performance area as rehearsed, but this time rehearse the song as well. Encourage the children to remember to:

  - concentrate and appear focussed on the performance;

  - look as though enjoying the performance;

  - perform with expression;

  - articulate the words clearly;

  - watch the conductor for cues (if you are using one).

- After the rehearsal, give positive feedback and encouragement.

3 Perform the song to an audience 🔊 8))

- Perform the song as rehearsed.

- Afterwards, discuss what went well. Ask the children what they considered to be the three best things about the performance.

Who knows?
Exploring musical processes

IT'S A START

1 **Discuss different starting points which inspire composition and suggest the starting point for *The society raffles***

- Discuss the different starting points composers use as the inspiration for their compositions, eg:
  - a picture, scene or mood;
  - the desire to express the way they feel;
  - an event, historical or current;
  - an expression of religious or social opinions and beliefs;
  - a film, play or television programme;
  - a poem, story or saying;
  - a melodic or rhythmic idea ...
- Divide the class into small groups. Each group makes a list of as many different starting points they can think of and writes down examples of pieces of music or songs they know for each.
- Each group shares their list with the rest of the class.
- All listen to *The society raffles* (track 14). Ask the children to suggest what the starting point for this composition might have been, indicating their reasons.

Vibraslap   Flexatone

Teaching tips
- Metre - how the beat is grouped, eg in waltz time the beat is grouped in threes: 1 2 3 1 2 3
- Timbre - quality of sound, eg hollow, squeaky.
- Tempo - the speed of music.
- Pitch - refers to the complete range of sounds in music from the lowest to the highest.

2 **Discuss ways in which *The society raffles* music reflects the movie for which it was composed**

- All watch *The society raffles* silent movie (videoclip 5) and listen to the music in context. Ask the children to suggest which came first, the music or the movie, indicating their reasons.
  (The movie came first; the music was composed to reflect what was happening in the movie.)
- All listen to *The society raffles* again (track 14). Ask what the main instrument is. *(Piano.)*

  Discuss which other sounds are used, and listen to track 15 to hear each sound played separately.
  (1 vibraslap, 2 two-tone woodblock, 3 low-pitched woodblock, 4 triangle, 5 flexatone, 6 swanee whistle, 7 shaker.)

  Discuss how the percussion sounds have been used to capture what is happening in the movie *(eg the flexatone adds humour to the bowing; the swanee whistle mimics the sitting down action ...).*

3 **Invent symbols to represent the percussion sounds in *The society raffles***

- Show the children *The society raffles* photocopiable. Explain that this depicts the key events in the movie as a storyboard.
- Explain that the grey box below the pictures is where the children will insert symbols to indicate when each of the sound effects occurs in the music.

  All listen again to the sound effects played on their own *(track 15)* and decide on suitable symbols to represent each sound, eg

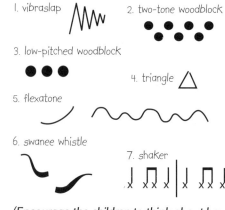

1. vibraslap
2. two-tone woodblock
3. low-pitched woodblock
4. triangle
5. flexatone
6. swanee whistle
7. shaker

(Encourage the children to think about how the symbol reflects the pitch and changes in pitch of the instrumental sound.)

- Watch the movie again, all tapping the beat using fingertips on knees, and counting the beats quietly *(each strong beat is count one).*

  Ask when the tempo of the music changes, and why.
  (It gets faster just before the end when the woman sees the burglar.)

  Discuss how the beats are grouped throughout *(the metre).*
  (There is a four-beat metre for the start, followed by a three-beat metre for most of the piece while the man is pretending to court the woman. This changes to a two-beat metre towards the end when the tempo gets faster.)

Background information
- Silent movies developed with the invention of the motion picture camera in 1895.
- Charlie Chaplin is the most famous silent movie actor.
- Music (usually a piano) normally accompanied silent movies.

The society raffles

Introduction

The Society Raffles
©December 7, 1905
American Mutoscope
& Biograph Company

Beginning section

Middle section

End section

SOUNDTRACK

1 **Complete the storyboard score for** *The society raffles*

- Revise *The society raffles* by watching the silent movie *(videoclip 5)*, then following the storyboard score on *The society raffles* photocopiable.

  Discuss the tempo and metre of the music in the three main sections marked on the score.
  (The beginning section has a four-beat metre; the middle section has a three-beat metre, and the end section has a two-beat metre and is faster.)

- Revise the symbols you decided on as a class for each of the sound effects *(Lesson 1, activity 3)*. Then, working as a class or in groups, watch the silent movie over and over to work out where the percussion sound effects occur.

  Write the symbols in the grey boxes on the storyboard score.
  (A sample answer sheet is available to download and print out from the CD-ROM if required.)

2 **Perform *The society raffles* using the storyboard score**

- Perform *The society raffles* from the class or an individual group's score using the ideas suggested below:

  - the action
    either show the silent movie without sound or invite four individuals (one for each of the four characters) to act out the movie;

  - the background music *(piano part)*
    a small group imitates the rhythms the piano played using tuned or untuned percussion making sure they maintain a steady beat throughout, including getting faster towards the end and making clear when the music has a metre of four, three or two beats;

  - the sound effects
    another group use their voices to imitate the percussion sounds.

3 **Listen to examples of music composed from a different starting point**

- Turn the sound off on your computer to watch the silent movie again, this time with a different musical accompaniment. Press play on your CD player at the same time as you start the silent movie for each of tracks 16 and 17.

  Discuss how well each track fits with the movie.
  *(Track 17 fits better because it has a lighter mood and a three-beat metre like the majority of **The society raffles**. However, neither track was written to accompany the movie. The aim of this activity is to reinforce how carefully the music for **The society raffles** was devised.)*

- Listen to *Fanfare for the common man (track 16)* again without the movie, and discuss the real inspiration for this piece of music.

  Ask how the composer conveys the theme of the music *(eg there is a serious and solemn mood and military fanfares)*.

- Listen to *Waltz* from *Serenade for strings (track 17)* again without the movie. Explain that this composition was inspired by a dance.

Background information

- *Fanfare for the common man* was composed in 1942 by Aaron Copland (1900-1990). It is a tribute to the Allied troups involved in World War II and is dedicated to all the 'ordinary people' who won no fame or glory in battle.

- *Waltz* from *Serenade for strings* was written by Peter Tchaikovsky (1840-93). As the title suggests it is performed only on string instruments - violins, violas, cellos and double basses.

MUSICAL CARTOONS

1 **Play the *Acting game* to rehearse ways to reflect a mime with music**

- Divide the class into pairs to devise a short mime to perform to the class *(eg everyday activities such as cleaning teeth, humorous mimes such as clowns splatting each other with a custard pie, a man slipping on a banana skin ...)*.

- Each pair rehearses their mime.

- Invite pairs to perform their mime to the class. For each mime, invite a volunteer to improvise vocal and/or body percussion sound effects to reflect the mime.
  (Some children might explore ways of using a xylophone or keyboard instead of voices and body percussion.)

  Discuss the imaginative ways in which the sound effects reflected the mime.

Teaching tips

- Write some of the ideas discussed on the board for the children to refer to as they plan their composition.

- Visit each of the groups as they are working and offer suggestions for improvement.

- Some groups may find it helpful to act out the cartoon to help them work out the timing of the sound effects.

2 **Compose music to represent a cartoon strip**

- Show the children the *Cartoon strip* photocopiable and discuss what is happening in each frame.

- Divide the children into groups and explain that each group will compose music to represent this cartoon. They first decide the outcome of the cartoon and fill in the final frame, without any other groups seeing their drawing.
  (Explain that the last frame could involve a different character.)

- Before the groups start working on their compositions discuss some of the important features the music will need to reflect, eg:

  - movement *(eg fast rhythm or melody for the dog running away; melody or rhythm slows down suddenly when the dog grinds to a halt ...)*;

  - each character's mood *(eg cheeky dog, angry man in the first frame; scared dog in the second frame ...)*;

  - sound effects *(eg the sound of the dog's paws as it slides to a halt)*.

- Discuss some musical considerations, eg:

  - tempo: will the speed be constant throughout or will it change, if so when?

  - metre: is there an overall metre for the piece, eg a waltzing three-beat feel; will the music change metre?

  - timbre: which sounds would best represent each character or event? *(eg voices, keyboard, tuned or untuned percussion instruments, sounds made using ICT ...)*

  - dynamics: will there be any sudden or gradual changes in volume?

  - pitch: high sounds or low sounds? *(eg deep/low sounds for the man, higher sounds for the dog)*

- Each group plans and rehearses their composition.

3 **Perform and appraise the cartoon compositions**

- Each group performs their cartoon composition to the rest of the class. Invite members of the class to suggest what happened at the end of the cartoon each time. Were they right?

  Appraise each composition, thinking in particular about:

  - how effectively the music conveyed what happened in the cartoon;

  - whether any instruments or sound effects were particularly well used;

  - whether each character's mood was conveyed throughout.

Cartoon strip

SCORE IT UP

1 **Watch a silent movie which will be the starting point for a group composition** 📹 6 pic 7

- All watch *Subub surprises the burglar (videoclip 6)*. Explain that the children are going to work in groups to compose music to accompany the movie. Explain that the music will:

  – accompany the dramatic action;

  – include appropriate sound effects;

  – convey the mood of the two characters throughout.

  Explain that the musical events will need to coincide precisely with events in the movie as in *The society raffles (Lesson 1 activity 2)*.

- Watch the silent movie several times for everyone to become really familiar with it, then divide the class into groups. Each group maps out the key events in the movie using words and/or pictures, eg:

  – burglar creeps in through the window;

  – burglar rummages through sleeping man's belongings;

  – quiet shock when man wakes up to see burglar in his room;

  – bed is pulled up against the wall;

  – shots from the bed;

  – burglar panics and then disappears in a puff of smoke;

  – bed drops back down;

  – man celebrates, dances on his bed.

  (A blank storyboard score for this silent movie is available to print out from the CD-ROM. There are nine boxes on the storyboard, but not all need to be filled.)

2 **Work out a plan of the silent movie and spot when sound effects should occur** 📹 6 pic 7

- Each group continues to map out the key events in *Subub surprises the burglar (filling in the storyboard score from the CD-ROM if desired)*.

- When each group has worked out the key events in the movie, they should watch the silent movie again several times to spot when specific events occur that would require a sound effect.

  Each group notes down their ideas on their group score.

- Invite each group to share their ideas with the class.

3 **Explore instrumental sounds to accompany the silent movie, *Subub surprises the burglar***

- The groups consider which instrumental sounds – timbres – would be suitable for their composition. Encourage them to explore:

  – classroom percussion sounds;

  – electronic keyboard sounds;

  – instruments from home;

  – electronic equipment sounds;

  – sounds created and/or modified using ICT ...

  Each group makes a note of their chosen sounds on their scores for next lesson.
  (Make sure groups include any computer or keyboard settings on their score so that they can find their chosen sounds again.)

Teaching tips

- Spotting - the technical term for working out the hit points in a movie where something needs to be emphasised in the music.

- If possible, groups should make a note of the seconds when a particular action occurs.

- It is up to the children what they spot, not every group will spot the same things.

- Groups do not have to hit every point of action, eg every item of clothing thrown on the floor. The music will be more effective if it is kept simple and uncluttered.

MUSIC FOR THE MOVIES

1 **Begin composing music in groups to accompany *Subub surprises the burglar*** 🎥 **6** 📷 **pic 7**

- All revise the work from last lesson on *Subub surprises the burglar (videoclip 6)*. Watch the silent movie then each group follows their notes on their group score.

- Encourage each group to think about the structure of their piece, eg:

  - does the movie have distinct sections *(eg beginning, middle and end)* which might be represented in the music?

  - does anything happen in the movie to indicate a change in mood, tempo or metre?

  - what will remain constant in the music to provide unity? *(eg the piano plays throughout in* **The society raffles***)*

  Each group makes a note of their ideas on their score.

- Each group begins trying out their ideas.

Teaching tips

- Give the children access to the videoclip throughout their preparation time so that they can carefully plan and develop their composition.

- Wherever possible, encourage children to use keyboards, microphones and computers to create interesting timbres and effects for their composition.

- Visit each group regularly to provide support.

- Encourage groups to be as imaginative as possible with their sound effects, exaggerating the humour subtly as well as obviously.

- Have copies of the **Subub and the burglar** blank storyboard score available for groups to use.

- Some groups may prefer to find their own way of representing their ideas as a score.

2 **Groups explore and refine ideas for their composition** 🎥 **6** 📷 **pic 7**

- Each group continues developing, rehearsing and refining ideas for their group composition.
  (Some groups may abandon many of their initial ideas as their composition unfolds. This is fine.)

- Encourage each group to appoint a conductor to help synchronise the music with the movie. The conductor might count the seconds out loud as they rehearse, as well as provide cues.

3 **Perform the work in progress to the class who suggest ways of improving it**

- Each group performs their work in progress to the class.

- The class offers encouragement and also suggests improvements. Think about:

  - whether the music follows the drama;

  - whether the sound effects are appropriate and well-synchronised;

  - whether the mood is well-represented throughout;

  - whether all members of the group are confident about what they are performing and when.

Teaching tips

- By sharing work in progress, the groups can provide inspiration to others.

- Encourage each group to make a note of ideas from the suggestions for improvement for next lesson.

- The children may find it useful to watch and discuss *The society raffles* silent movie *(videoclip 5)* to revise ideas the composer used. They might also like to revise the discussions about their cartoon strip compositions from lesson 3.

SUBUB SURPRISES THE BURGLAR

1 **Rehearse and refine the group compositions to accompany *Subub surprises the burglar***

• Each group rehearses their compositions following the suggestions from the class last lesson.

Remind the children that their composition should:

– follow the drama of what is happening in the silent movie;

– include appropriate sound effects;

– convey the mood of the two characters throughout;

– coincide precisely with events in the movie.

Teaching tips

• Help each group to work out whether their sound effects coincide precisely with the movie.

• If you have a computer-compatible projector, you could show the silent movie on a large screen so that the group performing can follow the movie and so that the rest of the class can watch.

• Ensure that the children watching the silent movie are not watching the musicians - this will help them to assess more carefully how effectively the music follows the action.

2 **Groups rehearse their compositions individually with the silent movie**

• Give each group the opportunity to work on their own with the silent movie (*videoclip 6*) so that they can practise synchronising their music with it.

Encourage each group to work out the best way for their conductor to help them synchronise the music with the silent movie.
(*The performers will find they are watching the movie sometimes and their conductor at other times.*)

3 **Perform and record each group's composition with the movie and appraise the result**

• As a class, watch the movie whilst listening to each group's accompaniment.

After each performance, invite members of the class to suggest the three best features of each group's composition, and discuss whether:

– the sound events occurred simultaneously with the events in the movie;

– the music captured the mood of the characters in the movie;

– the chosen instrumental timbres were effective in reflecting the movie.

Index

Videoclips

Track   Contents

NB There are also 15 videoclips for teachers
(see introduction p6)

Audio CD track list 🔊

Acknowledgements

The author and publishers would like to thank all the teachers and consultants who assisted in the preparation of this series: Meriel Ascott, Francesca Bedford, Chris Bryant, Rob Bullough, Yolanda Cattle, Veronica Clark, Kate Davies, Barry Gibson, Veronica Hanke, Jonty Harrison, Jocelyn Lucas, Helen MacGregor, Carla Moss, Danny Monte, Lio Moscardini, Sue Nicholls, Vanessa Olney, Mrs S. Pennington, Marie Penny, Pauline Quinton, Jane Sebba, Heather Scott, Michelle Simpson, Debbie Townsend and Joy Woodall.

The author and publishers would like to thank Vivien Ellis, Kevin Graal, Michael Haslam, Debbie Sanders and Cleveland Watkiss for performing on the recording of the CD.

Special thanks are due to Danny Monte and the Year 6 children of Brunswick Park Primary School for demonstrating and performing for the filming of the CD-ROM videoclips.

The following have kindly granted permission for the inclusion of their copyright materials and recordings in the book and on the CD:

Stephen Chadwick for the music of **Loopy weather, Crazy green bottles** and **The society raffles** © 2003 A & C Black Publishers Limited.

Ana Sanderson for the words and music of **Silver and gold** © 1997 A & C Black Publishers Limited.

Ana Sanderson for the words and music of **Relay race** © 2002 A & C Black Publishers Limited.

Universal Music for **Waltz** from **Serenade for Strings**, performed by The Netherlands Symphony Orchestra, directed by Zinman. Courtesy of Phillips Classics, part of the Universal Music Group.

BMG Music UK & Ireland for **Alpha** performed by Vangelis. Licensed courtesy of BMG UK & Ireland Ltd.

Hyperion Records Ltd for **Fanfare for the common man** by Aaron Copland cat. CDA66189, and for **Gnossienne no 3** by Eric Satie cat. CDA66365. Both used by courtesy of Hyperion Records Limited, London.

Malcolm Abbs for **I wanna sing scat** © 1995 Malcolm Abbs. Used with permission.

Sing for Pleasure for **Junkanoo** by Jan Holdstock, © Sing for Pleasure 0800 0184 164

Topic Records for **Bendrong** from CD **Flutes and Gamelan Music of West Java** – Topic TSCD913. Released under license from Topic Records Limited. www.topicrecords.co.uk

Art of Landscape for **Winds on the mountain** performed by Incantation © Art of Landscape 1982.

Columbia Records for **Goodbye now** by Brownie McGhee. From cassette 476683 4 **Hard times and heartaches**. The **Roots 'n' Blue** collection. Courtesy Columbia Records and for **Hard times blues** by Buddy Moss from cassette 472191 4 **The slide guitar – bottles knives and steel** vol 2. Courtesy of Columbia Records.

King Record Co. Ltd, Japan for **Gamelan gong keb yar of 'Ka Cita'** (Baris gede 'bandrangan') Abian Kapas Kaja from © CD KICC 5154 – licensed by King Record Co. Tokyo, Japan.

All other recordings are © 2003 A &C Black and ℗ 2003 A & C Black.

The following copyright holders have kindly given their permission for the inclusion of their copyright material on the CD-ROM:

The **gamelan** photographs are courtesy of Norfolk Music Education Service.

The society raffles and **Subub surprises the burglar** courtesy of Library of Congress, American Memory Historical Collection.
All videoclips are © A & C Black

Music Express Year 6 CD and CD-ROM © and ℗ 2003 A & C Black Publishers Ltd. All rights of the owner of the works reproduced reserved. Unauthorised copying, hiring, lending, public performance and broadcasting of these recordings and videoclips prohibited.

Every effort has been made to trace and acknowledge copyright owners. If any right has been omitted, the publishers offer their apologies and will rectify this in subsequent editions following notification.